THE
ALBIGENSIAN
CRUSADES

THE ALBIGENSIAN CRUSADES

Joseph R. Strayer

With a New Epilogue by Carol Lansing

Ann Arbor Paperbacks

THE UNIVERSITY OF MICHIGAN PRESS

First edition as an Ann Arbor Paperback 1992
Epilogue, second appendix, and bibliographic supplement
copyright © by the University of Michigan 1992
Copyright © 1971 by the estate of Joseph R. Strayer
All rights reserved
Published in the United States of America by
The University of Michigan Press
Manufactured in the United States of America

2000   8   7

Library of Congress Cataloging-in-Publication Data

Strayer, Joseph Reese, 1904–
     The Albigensian Crusades / Joseph R. Strayer ; with a new epilogue
by Carol Lansing.
          p.   cm. — (Ann Arbor paperbacks)
     Reprint. Originally published: New York : Dial Press, 1971.
     Includes bibliographical references and index.
     ISBN 0-472-09476-9 (alk. paper). — ISBN 0-472-06476-2 (pbk. :
alk. paper)
     1. Albigenses—History. 2. France, Southwest—History—Religious
aspects. 3. France—Church history—Middle Ages, 987–1515.
I. Title.
DC83.3.S87 1992
944′.023—dc20   92-19755
                                                            CIP

Contents

124662

THE
ALBIGENSIAN
CRUSADES

The Albigensian Crusades slash through the history of France and of the Church like a gaping wound. From 1208 to 1226 the papacy sent army after army to the South of France to crush the Albigensian heretics and to punish their supporters. The Albigensian Crusades were religious wars and like all religious wars they were bloody and cruel. They began with a calculated act of terror, the massacre of Béziers; they ended with the establishment of the Inquisition, one of the most effective means of thought control that Europe has ever known. They were completely successful: The losing faith, the Albigensian heresy, was exterminated. The effects of the victory were lasting: The religious unity of Western Europe, the leadership of the Church, and the papal monarchy were preserved for many generations. Except for the Hussites of Bohemia, who lived on the very fringe of the Catholic world, the Church was not again seriously threatened by heresy until the rise of Luther in the early sixteenth century.

Successful wars, however, usually have unexpected consequences, and the Albigensian Crusades were no exception to this rule. For one thing, they made France a Mediterranean power and the greatest power in Europe. Before the Crusades, the king of France had no authority in the southern third of his country, no seaports on the Mediterranean, no direct contacts with Spain or Italy. Moreover, he showed no desire to move toward the South. It had been all that he could do to establish his control over the North and he was still consolidating his position there in the early 1200's. It was the Crusades that forced the king to take an interest in the South. The crusading armies were almost entirely composed of men from northern France; their leaders were royal vassals. The king avoided involvement in their campaigns as long as he could, but when the first phase of the Crusades ended in a stalemate he felt that he had to intervene. He did not want princes who were heretics, or at least fellow travelers, as his neighbors, and his own vassals had proved unable to govern the region or to extinguish heresy. So he invaded the South and annexed a great block of territory, running from the Pyrenees to the Rhône. It was this annexation that made France for the next five centuries the most powerful, the wealthiest, and the most populous state in Europe. Neither the pope nor the crusaders who answered his summons had planned to increase the authority of the French king, and yet the aggrandizement of France was one of the most durable results of the Crusades.

Conversely, the success of the Crusades led in the long run to the weakening of the papacy. If religious dissent could be crushed by the sword, then political dissent—disobedience to the pope—could also be crushed by the sword. Thirteenth-century popes were quick to draw this conclusion. They were also quick to draw another conclusion: Since the French royal family was responsible for final victory in the Albigensian Crusades, then the French royal family should take responsibility for other wars initiated by the papacy. The French were willing, if they were paid for their trouble, and the Church became dangerously dependent on French support. When, at the end of the thirteenth century, a French king quarreled with Pope Boniface VIII, the pope found that he was helpless. No one came to his aid, even when he was captured and insulted by a French-led gang of conspirators. The successor of Boniface did not dare to live in Italy; he had to take refuge at Avignon, on the borders of France. There the popes remained for over seventy years, improving their administrative apparatus and losing much of their spiritual prestige. They had wiped out heresy, they had defeated most of their political enemies, but they now had only lukewarm support from their friends. The fourteenth-century Church was far weaker, far less influential, than the thirteenth-century Church, and the weakness persisted until the period of the Reformation.

The rise of France, the weakening of the Church, were important events in European history. We would be living in a very different world if France had never acquired a Mediterranean coast; Napoleon, in such a case, almost certainly would not have been a French general. We would be living in a very different world if the Church had not weakened itself in the thirteenth century by becoming addicted to holy wars; in such a case there might not have been a Protestant Reformation. But beyond these obvious conclusions there is a difficult and perplexing problem. The Albigensian Crusades, and their aftermath, the Inquisition, offer one of the classic examples of repression of dissent and of freedom of thought. What effect did this repression have on Western Europe?

One unfortunate result was that secular governments learned how easy it was to suppress opposition to their policies. Very few men fought for any length of time in the crusading armies; even fewer men were needed to staff the Inquisition. Yet these small groups were able to wipe out a belief that was held by hundreds of thousands of men and that was viewed with some sympathy by hundreds of thousands of others. Continuing pressure, the use of torture, the imposition of social and economic disabilities, and a nicely graded set of penalties that encouraged the weak to betray the strong in return for immunity or token punishments were the techniques that led to the disintegration of the heretical sects. All these techniques were used by European states of the later Middle Ages. Modern totalitarian governments have made few innovations; they have simply been more efficient.

On the other hand, the cruelty of the Crusades and the injustices of the Inquisition caused large numbers of men to lose faith in both religious and secular institutions. Many good Catholics opposed the Crusades and thought of them as hypocritical excuses for a North French war of conquests. Many good Catholics hated the Inquisition and considered it merely a device for seizing the property of reputable citizens. There was no chance for open rebellion after 1250, but there was plenty of room for obstructionism, cynical political manipulations, and general apathy. When Western European society came under severe strains in the fourteenth century as a result of economic depression, political mismanagement, and plague, a very considerable part of the population made no effort to preserve or reform threatened institutions such as the Catholic Church or the kingdom of France. Instead, they merely tried to save their own status and income. Many forces converged to produce this indifference and this selfishness, but certainly one of the contributing causes was the bitter memory of the Albigensian Crusades. Repression can destroy a faith; it can also produce dangerous decay in the society that uses it.

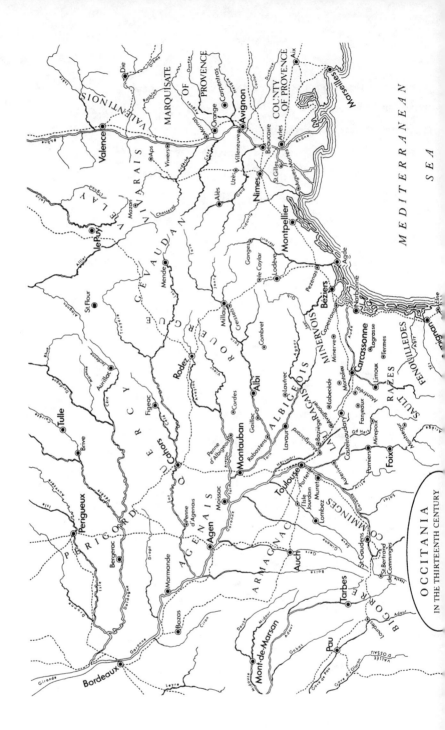

OCCITANIA
IN THE THIRTEENTH CENTURY

OCCITANIA

The country that we now call France did not exist in the early Middle Ages. Taken in its widest meaning, "France" included the territories lying between the Loire, the middle part of the Meuse, and the Scheldt. Taken in its narrowest sense, "France" was the Ile de France, the region around Paris. But no one thought that "France," wide or narrow, included the lands lying south of the Loire, and especially not the lands south of the Massif Central, the mountainous region that stretches from Lyons on the Rhône to the western coastal plain. Even in the fourteenth century, men spoke of journeying from Toulouse or Montpellier to "France."

There was a *rex Francorum*—a king of the Franks—who reigned not only in "France," but also in the lands south of the Loire. But he had very limited power in the lands that recognized him as king, even in the North. Down to 1200 he had practically no influence in Brittany or Normandy, which is why these principalities were often not thought of as part of

"France." He had more influence in Flanders, yet in the end most of Flanders escaped his grasp and became part of the Habsburg domains (and eventually of the kingdom of Belgium). His relations with Champagne and with the duchy of Burgundy were reasonably good, but again, he had no direct authority in either province in the twelfth or early thirteenth century. Nevertheless, the group of states just mentioned did have a common culture, and they were members, even if quarreling members, of the same political family. There were local dialects but no sharp language barriers; there were differences among provincial customs but none that were utterly incomprehensible to men who knew the general principles of their own law; there were constant conflicts between the states but no abiding hatreds. Members of the privileged classes felt at home almost anywhere in the North. Practically every great family (including the royal family) had at one time or another been allied to each of the other great families, and the possibility of renewing such alliances was always present. In short, while the North was politically fragmented, it was, in a sense, one country, and it did not seem impossible to hope for its eventual unification.

The situation in the South was different. It is not surprising that the king had little power in the large principalities such as Aquitaine and Toulouse, nor is it surprising that the was losing even nominal authority in the frontier counties of the Spanish March (which were to go to the crown of Aragon). A king who could not control Normandy could scarcely be expected to rule Toulouse; a king who could not keep Flanders within the realm could hardly preserve claims to lands beyond the Pyrenees. The significant difference was that the South did not form part of the cultural and political community of the northern states. It spoke its own language; it followed its own customs; its social and political structure was very unlike that of the North. In short, the South was a separate country, united to the North only in its recognition of a common king.

The differences between South and North ran so deep that they could not be ignored by even casual observers. The linguistic break between the French of the North and the Provençal (or Occitan, as many scholars prefer to call it) of the South is one of the sharpest in the whole family of Romance languages. The southern tongue is very close to Catalan, fairly close to Castilian, and quite remote from French. A merchant from Narbonne would have been easily understood in Barcelona, while he would have needed an interpreter in Paris. Moreover, while the upper classes in England and western Germany accepted French as the language of aristocratic society, the upper classes of the South did not. A baron of the Ile de France would have found more men to talk to in London, or even in Cologne, than he would have in Toulouse. Now a language barrier is not an impassable obstacle, but it is a real one, and it is the kind of barrier that creates misunderstandings and suspicions.

One reason for the difference between French and Provençal/Occitan was that the southern language was closer to Latin.

The same remark could be made about the differences between the customs of the two regions. One could scarcely call the laws of the South Roman, but they were more influenced by reminiscences of Roman law than were the customary laws of the northern principalities. It is also true that, as the revived study of Roman law spread from Italy across the Alps, men trained in Roman law made a conscious effort to introduce its principles into the courts of Aquitaine, Toulouse, and Provence, and to reinforce the Roman traditions that still survived in southern law. Great respect was given to men who knew Roman law; they often were asked to speak first in meetings and councils, even when counts and nobles were present. Their ideas were usually accepted and the divergence between the law of Paris and the law of the South grew rather than diminished during the twelfth century.

It is easier to be precise about differences in language and law than about differences in social behavior. Superficially, the South looked rather like the North: A class of noble landholders connected by feudal ties ruled and exploited a mass of free and unfree peasants; the upper clergy, recruited largely from aristocratic families, were also wealthy and powerful landholders; the bourgeoisie was gaining wealth and rights of municipal self-government. In fact, none of these generalizations is entirely accurate. Many members of the nobility had little or no land, because southern custom prescribed equal division of inheritances among all direct heirs. A man who was lord of one thirty-second of a castle or one sixteenth of a village could not be a local tyrant or an exploiting landlord. Many such nobles lived in towns; some of them engaged in business; some of them entered professions such as the law. Because of the large number of nobles and the fragmentation of their holdings, feudal ties had become almost meaningless. Most vassals had many lords and were not especially loyal to any of them; most vassals provided no significant service to their superiors. The landholding class did exploit the peasants, but by rather different methods than in the North. Integrated agricultural units like the manor were rare; there was relatively little demesne land and hence small demand for labor services; even serfs were more apt to find their disability marked by large payments to the lord than by heavy burdens of week-work. In short, the system was designed to produce a cash income rather than produce to be consumed or sold by the lord.

What has been said of the nobility could also be said of the higher clergy. Some abbots were a little more successful than their lay cousins in keeping extensive rural domains, but the bishops looked largely toward the towns. They tried to preserve or extend their property rights and their jurisdiction in the rapidly growing urban centers. Where they were successful they notably increased their income, but often they found themselves engaged in a three-cornered fight with nobles and burghers for control of a town. Sometimes, as at Narbonne, there was a division of authority among the three groups; but sometimes, as at Toulouse, the burghers gained the leading position; and sometimes, as at Montpellier, a noble family gained predominance. Overall, the result was that the southern prelates were weaker and poorer than those of many other regions. The bishop of Toulouse, who lived in one of the richest cities of the South, was one of the most impoverished prelates in the kingdom. In 1200 he had to ask the canons of his cathedral to furnish him a daily allowance of food, and he could visit the churches of his diocese only by imploring the help of neighboring lords. Other bishops were better off and were accused of being scandalously wealthy, offensively luxurious, and cruelly greedy, but wealth and luxury are relative terms. What seemed like great wealth to a middle-class merchant would not have impressed an archbishop of Rouen or of Reims. As for greed, it was poverty rather than wealth that drove the southern prelates to assert and defend their rights so vigorously. In a country where, as we shall see, there was little effective government, a bishop had to be fairly tough just to hold his own.

It is obvious that the South was more urbanized than the North, but the difference goes deeper than a mere variation in the percentage of town dwellers. The southerners thought in urban terms even when they lived in the country; the northerners thought in rural terms even when they lived in towns. The most striking example of this state of mind is the way in which southern peasants imitated urban institutions. Villages of a few hundred souls had their own officials, and their public assemblies; they tried, not always successfully, to secure recognition as corporate bodies. If this was the program of the peasantry, one can imagine what were the aspirations of the bourgeoisie. Every town sought a maximum degree of autonomy with full power to govern and to protect its inhabitants. Every town tried to reduce the power of its lord to purely ceremonial acts. The movement was almost irresistible. By 1200 the greatest lord in the South, the count of Toulouse, had yielded almost all power in his own capital city to the consuls, the leaders of the bourgeoisie.

In many ways, the southern towns resembled the rising city-states of Italy. Noble landowners and knights frequently lived within the town walls and took part in the town government. The larger and stronger towns encouraged and at times almost forced landed aristocrats to become citizens and to assume the responsibilities of citizenship. Knights formed a considerable part of the armed forces of the city of Toulouse. At Nîmes the governing body of the town was composed of four knights and four members of the bourgeoisie. If the nobles could not be persuaded to live in the town they might be pushed into becoming vassals of the town. Toulouse had a number of noble vassals who owed it military service and it was usually more successful in securing that service than the ordinary feudal lord was. The military power that resulted from a combination of burghers and knights enabled the towns to dominate the rural areas around them. Just before 1200 Toulouse was clearly trying to gain control of the castles that might threaten its main trade routes and the villages that supplied it with food. It made alliances, wars, and treaties just as

7

a feudal lord would have done; it beat down competitors and secured free passage of its exports over a large part of the Southwest.

In all these respects the South differed from the France of the North. In the North knights and burgesses were sharply separated both in function and in habitat. A town might owe militia service to a lord; a lord almost never owed service to a town. The authority of a town ended sharply at its walls, or at a fixed line a mile or so beyond the walls. A town had no right, and very seldom the opportunity, to engage in political expansion or military aggression. To a northern knight the behavior of southern towns was outrageous, which may be one reason why northern knights proved so willing to attack the South.

With urbanism went a certain amount of cosmopolitanism. Foreigners and unbelievers were not only tolerated, they were often completely absorbed into the society. Jews suffered hardly any disabilities in the towns along the Mediterranean coast. They could practice their professions; and they could (which was even rarer in a Christian country) own large amounts of land. There was no discrimination against the heretics who began to be numerous in the twelfth century; they had all the rights of any inhabitant of the country. Certainly there was more prejudice against the Moslems, but this prejudice did not extend to Moslem learning or Moslem literature. The writings of Moslem doctors were respected in the medical school that was beginning to form in Montpellier, and Moorish poetry clearly had an influence on the form and content of Provençal poetry.

This brings us to our last point of difference between the two regions. Literature may not always reflect exactly the ideals and interests of a society, but in the twelfth century it probably came fairly close to doing so. During this period there were great writers in both French and Provençal/Occitan. During the first half of the twelfth century the preferred form in the North was the epic, in the South the lyric. One theme was common to both—praise of bravery, joy in battle. But the range of the southern writers was wider—they sang of the bittersweet experiences of love; they commented, often savagely, on current events; they challenged each other to literary duels; they satirized their contemporaries. All these themes appeared eventually in the North, but the South clearly had the lead in these sophisticated, highly individualistic genres. Finally, while we know very little about the men who wrote in French in the early twelfth century, we know a great deal about the southern poets. It is interesting that they stand out as individuals; it is equally interesting that many of them were members of the nobility. It was to be some years before northern barons felt any desire to write verses.

To repeat, the North and the South of what is now France were, in the twelfth century, two different countries, as different as France and Spain are today. The people of each country disliked and distrusted those of the other. The northerners thought that the southerners were undisciplined, spoiled by luxury, a little soft, too much interested in social graces, too much influenced by contemptible people such as businessmen, lawyers, and Jews. The southerners thought the northerners were crude, arrogant, discourteous, uncultured, and aggressive. The climate of opinion was such that if a war were to break out between the two countries it was sure to be long and bitter.

While the northern country had a name, France, the southern country had no name; it was too fragmented politically to have accepted any one regional name as a general appelation.[1] After the French conquest of the thirteenth century a large section of the country was called Languedoc because in the southern language "oc" was used instead of "oui" to mean "yes." But Languedoc never included all of the South and eventually it was applied only to the districts of Toulouse, Carcassonne-Béziers, and Beaucaire-Nîmes. Moreover, it was not a name that the men of the South would have given themselves, though they accepted it in the end. As such, it does not seem appropriate to use it to describe the South during its period of independence. I have decided therefore to use an artificial name for the South, derived, like Languedoc, from the southern language. I propose to call it Occitania. Occitania would include all the regions in which Occitan was spoken, all

---

[1] This fact embarrassed both the papal curia and the French royal court. In papal letters the region was usually called Provence, from the name of its easternmost district, the one that lay closest to Italy. Royal letters usually spoke of Albigeois, a small part of the county of Toulouse where heretics were especially numerous.

the regions that possessed the customs and the social and political patterns that were common to the South and strange to the North.

Occitania was a country; it was not a state or even a loose federation of states. Parts of Occitania were so politically fragmented that they were practically ungovernable; and even in the more unified areas the authority of the overlords was precarious. The country can be divided roughly into five subregions, each of which had a very different fate. The northwest and the west were part of the duchy of Aquitaine, a duchy held after 1152 by the kings of England. The strong Anglo-Norman tradition of government was considerably attenuated by the time that it reached the basin of the lower Garonne, but it was still strong enough so that Aquitaine was spared some of the troubles of the rest of Occitania. Heresy did not reach major proportions in the lands held of the king of England and only the fringes of his domains were touched by the Albigensian Crusades.

The Pyrenees and the plains near the foot of the Pyrenees were held by a group of counts who were very nearly independent princes. Some were vassals of the duke of Aquitaine, some of the count of Toulouse, but neither ruler had much authority over the lords of the Pyrenees. It required a major effort to capture castles perched on rocky peaks above the narrow gorges of mountain streams, and there was always a danger that a campaign in the Pyrenees would stir up a reaction in

Spain. The king of Aragon, in particular, had claims to lands in Occitania, and some of the mountain counts held fiefs from him, as well as from Toulouse. If the lords of the Pyrenees had held together, they might have escaped the storms of the thirteenth century almost unscathed, but they agreed no better than the other inhabitants of the country. Several of them were singed by the Albigensian wars; one, the count of Foix, was badly burned.

The northern region of Occitania, the Massif Central, was also a mountainous area. Like the Pyrenees, it was divided among many more or less independent lords; unlike the Pyrenees, some of its most important lords were ecclesiastics. Thus the bishop of Mende was count of Gévaudan, and the bishops of Viviers and Le Puy were the dominant lords in their counties. All three bishops claimed extensive rights of government; in fact, down to 1307 the bishop of Mende argued that he was sovereign in his county. Farther west, the bishop of Rodez was at least as powerful as the count of Rouergue (which isn't saying much), and some of the monasteries in the region also had a considerable degree of autonomy. The importance of ecclesiastical lordships, and the isolation and the poverty of the Massif Central, helped to protect it against the worst violences of the Crusades. Like Aquitaine, only the edges were seriously damaged.

Across the Rhône, in the southeast corner of Occitania, lay the county of Provence. In language and in culture it was indistinguishable from the lands to the west of the Rhône; in fact,

Provençal and Occitan are almost interchangeable names for what is essentially the same language. But Provence had the great good fortune to be technically part of a different kingdom, the kingdom of Burgundy. The kingdom of Burgundy, in turn, was one of the realms of the Holy Roman Emperor. Now, from the death of the emperor Henry VI in 1197 to the death of Conrad IV in 1254 the popes were involved in a complicated pattern of negotiation and struggle with the emperors. In imperial lands the problem of the Empire clearly took precedence over the problem of heresy. Crusades in the Empire were preached against recalcitrant emperors and their allies, rather than against heretics. Thus, while Provence certainly was not free from heresy, the Albigensian Crusades barely touched the region; the city of Avignon was the only place in Provence that really suffered from the war.

There remains the heartland of Occitania, the great arc of territory that ran from the borders of Aquitaine through Toulouse, Carcassonne, Béziers, Narbonne, Montpellier, and Nîmes over to the Rhône. This region contained some of the richest land and some of the wealthiest cities of the whole country. Almost all of it was subject, directly or indirectly, to the count of Toulouse, and he drew the largest part of his revenues from this area. Nevertheless, even this heartland of Occitania was far from forming a political unit. The count did not control the largest cities. Toulouse was self-governing; Narbonne was divided between the archbishop and the viscount; the greater part of Montpellier was held by a local dynasty whose rights in 1202 passed to the royal house of Aragon. Even worse, squarely in the midst of the count's domains lay the holdings of the Trencavel family, stretching from Carcassonne and Béziers in the south to Albi in the north and including a number of strongly fortified places. The Trencavel were ambitious, aggressive, brave, and (for the most part) utterly lacking in political sense. They could not be controlled and they would not let themselves be ignored. No other vassals of the count of Toulouse were quite as unruly, but there were not many men on whom he could rely in times of trouble. Each important noble family was trying to build up its power in its own lands; it was not concerned with strengthening the central government of the county or even with increasing general security. The count of Toulouse was accepted as a sort of symbolic leader of Occitania and his presence was felt everywhere. He had lands scattered throughout the region, including extensive holdings in Provence; he had vassals even in the remote areas of the northern and southern mountains. But the count of Toulouse was a symbol of a shared culture, not of a shared political experience. Neither Occitania as a whole, nor the county of Toulouse, nor any lesser unit was integrated or organized well enough either to discipline its own people or to resist strong outside pressures. This political weakness made possible the success of the Albigensian Crusades.

II

THE HERETICS

It is easy to see that in a country with no effective political organization it would be difficult to wipe out heretical movements. It is less easy to see why Occitania was so receptive to heretical doctrines. Most of the reasons given for the attractiveness of heresy to the people of Occitania apply equally well to people of other countries. But in the twelfth and thirteenth centuries the only other country that was seriously infected with heresy was northern Italy. In Germany and northern France there were only small groups of heretics and in England there were almost none.

Geography gives some help, but no conclusive answers. Occitania was close to the original center of one major heresy—Waldensianism—and on a main line of dispersion of the other major heresy—Catharism. It is not surprising that the followers of Peter Waldo of Lyons should have spread south and west into Occitania. But why did the Waldensians have less success in spreading north? Again, it is perfectly understandable how

Catharism could spread from Bulgaria to Bosnia, from Bosnia to northern Italy, and from northern Italy to Occitania. But why does the current of spreading heresy slow down almost exactly at the border between Occitania and France? We were told long ago that "heresy follows the routes of trade" and one of the greatest trade routes of the Middle Ages ran up the Rhône to Champagne and the Ile de France. Heresy did follow this route, but lost its vigor when it entered French-speaking lands. The heretics of the North were less numerous, less confident, less well organized than those of the South. Why could they flourish in an Occitanian environment and not in a French one?

An old, but often repeated answer to the problem emphasizes the corruption and lack of zeal in the clergy of Occitania. These depraved men, it is said, were so unfit for their tasks and so neglectful of their duties that they allowed the heretics to take over spiritual leadership by default. There is no doubt that the Church was corrupt in Occitania, but one can legitimately doubt whether it was more corrupt there than elsewhere.

In fact, there is little evidence against the Occitanian clergy in the first decade of the thirteenth century, except for rhetorical statements by popes and provincial councils. Doubtless there was some truth behind the rhetoric, but the same rhetoric was used in Paris, in Rouen, and in Oxford. Everywhere the clergy were accused of being worldly and avaricious, of keeping mistresses and wasting the wealth of their churches, of neglecting their duties and fleecing their parishioners. It was at Paris, not at Narbonne, that priests were accused of refusing to bury the dead until heavy fees were paid. It was at Toul, not Toulouse, that a deposed bishop stabbed his successor to death. It was a northern preacher, Geoffroi de Troyes, who said that the clergy differed from laymen only in dress, not in behavior, that they were hypocrites, ravening wolves in sheep's clothing. Even the habit of acting as a lawyer in order to gain wealth was not peculiar to Occitania; this practice was denounced at Poitiers and at Rouen as well as at Montpellier.

It is true that most of the parish priests of Occitania were ignorant, even, in some cases, functionally illiterate, and that they could not hold their own in arguments with heretics. But the same could have been said about parish priests, especially rural parish priests, in all parts of Europe. There were no seminaries in which to train them, no general standards that they had to meet. They were named to their posts by the men, usually laymen, who possessed the patronage of the parish, and the patrons were often more concerned about siphoning off some of the income of the Church than about the qualifications of a priest. Conscientious bishops of the thirteenth century kept records of their investigations of the parish clergy; the impression given by these records is appalling. Many priests knew scarcely enough Latin to say Mass; many, perhaps for this reason, shirked their duties. Many were drunkards or gamblers; in some dioceses practically all priests had concubines (in effect, wives) or mistresses. Yet our best evidence for a corrupt and ignorant parish clergy comes precisely from areas that were almost untouched by heresy, such as Normandy and England. The earliest records come from the diocese of Lincoln, where the bishops again and again had to order priests to attend school in order to learn a little Latin, or give bonds that they would abandon their concubines. Eudes Rigaud, who became archbishop of Rouen in 1248, found literally hundreds of priests who were unfit. Compared to his reports of violence, sottishness, lust, and stupidity, the Occitanian clergy seem almost model pastors. It is certainly true that the bishops of Lincoln and the archbishop of Rouen worried more about the character of their parish priests than did the bishops of Occitania, and that many scandals in the South were simply not reported. Nevertheless, there seems to be very little correlation between the low character of the parish clergy and susceptibility to heresy.

On the other hand, there does seem to be some reason to believe that the bishops of Occitania were less efficient and less zealous than those of northern France or England. Lack of energy, lack of administrative ability, preoccupation with problems of preserving secular rights and income distracted their attention from the problem of heresy and made them almost incapable of dealing with it even when they noticed it. Papal rhetoric should never be taken at face value, but Innocent III was not greatly exaggerating when he said that the archbishop of Narbonne and his suffragans were "blind men, dumb dogs who can no longer bark . . . men who will do anything for

18

money. All of them, from the greatest to the least are zealous in avarice, lovers of gifts, seekers of rewards. They justify the evil-doer for bribes and deny justice to the righteous. Through such men the name of the Lord is blasphemed among the people. . . . They say the good is bad and the bad is good; they turn light into darkness and darkness into light, sweet to bitter and bitter to sweet. They do not fear God nor respect man. . . . They give church offices to illiterate boys whose behavior is often scandalous. Hence the insolence of the heretics, the scorn of rulers and people for God and the Church. . . ."

Innocent went on to say that "The chief cause of all these evils is the archbishop of Narbonne, whose god is money, whose heart is in his treasury, who is concerned only with gold. This man, in his ten years as archbishop, has never visited his province, or even his diocese. Though he received his own consecration freely, he blushes to give anything freely; he demanded five hundred shillings from the bishop of Maguelonne before he would consecrate him. . . ."

In this letter, Innocent put his finger on a serious weakness when he accused the archbishop of never visiting the churches of his province or diocese. This was a common fault of the bishops of Occitania, and their negligence certainly made it easier for heretics to spread their doctrines. The fact that Innocent found it necessary to suspend four prelates from their functions—the archbishop of Narbonne, and the bishops of Toulouse, Béziers and Viviers—shows how seriously he took their failure.

The weakness of the bishops, however, was only in part due to their personal faults; it reflected, in many ways, the weakness of Occitanian society. In countries that had achieved some degree of centralization and that had strong rulers, bishops were usually men of considerable ability and they were usually supported wholeheartedly by lay authorities. We remember the spectacular quarrels between kings and popes; we forget that the normal pattern of Church-State relations ranged from healthy competition to close cooperation. A king of England rewarded only his most competent officials with nominations to bishoprics; such men could administer their dioceses efficiently and could count on the assistance of the king and their colleagues in the government if they met any serious opposition. If the pope succeeded, as he did from time to time, in naming one of his intimates to an English see, he was almost forced to pick a man of ability who could hold his own with colleagues who had been trained in the royal court. England, which had one of the most efficient secular governments of the Middle Ages, also had one of the best organized churches.

Occitania lay at the other extreme. No one lord had overriding influence in ecclesiastical appointments; no court was active enough to serve as a training ground for future bishops. Lay influence on the choice of bishops was exerted by petty dynasts who were seeking to augment family income, not to secure capable administrators for their lands. At best the bishops represented the interests of a small region; at worst they represented the triumph of one local faction over another.

They could not cooperate effectively with each other; they could not easily think in terms of the common welfare of Occitania, much less in terms of the welfare of Christendom. The papacy was, to some extent, aware of this weakness, but the papacy had more serious problems to face in the twelfth century. It was threatened by the ambitions of Hohenstaufen emperors and Plantagenet kings, by the quarrels of Roman nobles and the rebellions of the Roman mob. It mattered a great deal who was archbishop of Milan, of Cologne, of Reims, of Canterbury. It mattered a good deal less who was archbishop of Narbonne. The papacy kept a careful eye on ecclesiastical appointments in northern Italy, northern France, Germany, and England. It was much less concerned about appointments in Occitania.

But while the weakness of the Occitanian episcopate helps to explain the lack of organized resistance to heresy, it does not explain the willingness of the people to accept heresy. There were many other regions where bishops were unable to administer their dioceses effectively (Ireland, for example) but not all these regions were centers of heresy. Fortunately for the Church, zeal for the faith does not depend on the excellence of administrative systems.

Here we come to the heart of the problem: The people of Occitania had lost much of their zeal, much of their devotion to the faith. We shall never know the exact figures, but it is probable that even at the peak of their success the heretics, avowed or concealed, were only a minority of the population.

But the Catholic majority seemed unconcerned about the threat that the growth of heresy posed to the Church. It showed no aversion to men who were trying to subvert one of the fundamental institutions of society. Catholics and heretics lived side by side in complete friendship; Catholic families seldom disowned a relative who became a herètic. In fact, many of the great noble families had one or more heretics among their members and these heretics, especially if they were women, were treated with great respect. In the same way, heresy had no dangerous political consequences. Lords did not try to use charges of heresy to dispossess their vassals, and towns did not bar heretics from municipal office. Toulouse, one of the largest and richest cities of Occitania, frequently chose heretics as consuls, that is, as members of its governing council.

Even more startling were the public disputations that were held between Catholic bishops and leaders of the heretics. These debates seem to have been enjoyed by men from all ranks of society; no one was shocked by the strong, even indecent attacks made by the heretics against the doctrine and the structure of the Church of Rome. Thus in 1207 St. Dominic himself had to hear a heretical leader argue that the "Roman Church is the devil's church and her doctrines are those of demons, she is the Babylon whom St. John called the mother of fornication and abomination, drunk with the blood of saints and martyrs . . . neither Christ nor the apostles has established the existing order of the mass." The judges of the debate were (typically for the region) two knights and two burgesses;

equally typically, they made no decision, but let everyone form his own opinion. In short, the general feeling seems to have been that the heretics were good men, that they had interesting ideas, that people who accepted these ideas were doing nothing wrong or foolish, that heresy was not a serious problem.

As these attitudes appear reasonable in a world that has accepted religious toleration, it may be hard to realize how peculiar and shocking they seemed to men of the twelfth century. We might remember that we show a good deal less tolerance about differences in political belief, probably because we feel that the good life here on earth depends more on political organization than on religious orthodoxy. But for the vast majority of medieval men life on this earth was short and harsh. Even with the increase in production and in security that had occurred in the twelfth century, the most fortunate still had no protection against sudden disasters and the least fortunate lived lives of abject misery. The good life in this world was an impossibility; the one real hope was the blessed life of those who were called to salvation. The Church, and the Church alone, could put men on the path to salvation. Only by believing the eternal truths taught by the Church, only by receiving the sacraments administered by the Church, could men be saved. Anyone who denied these truths, anyone who repudiated the sacraments, anyone who sought to destroy the Church was an enemy of mankind, a murderer who sought to kill the immortal soul rather than the earthly body. No weakness in the Church could excuse such a crime. The doctrine of the Church was pure even if her ministers were not; the sacraments were efficacious even if administered by sinful priests. The one unforgivable offense was to persist in heresy after the error had been demonstrated. It was the duty of all men to combat heresy, according to their understanding and station in life. Failure to fight heresy was as evil as heresy itself.

Yet it is perfectly evident that a large part of the population of Occitania did not want to fight heresy. We can only speculate about the causes of this indifference. Occitania, especially eastern Occitania, had been one of the earliest Latin-speaking regions to accept Christianity; it had not lagged far behind Italy. It had produced saints and scholars, and it had founded some of the first monasteries in the West, monasteries that were a model for all its neighbors. But this early fervor for the faith had dwindled in later centuries and nothing had happened to revive it. Occitanians had led no important religious movement and had participated only lukewarmly in movements led by men from other regions. For instance, Occitania had taken little part in the great missionary drive that converted the eastern Germans, the Scandinavians, and the Slavs. Occitania had been only slightly touched by the monastic reformers of the tenth and eleventh cenuries; even its neighbors at Cluny had not made much impression on the country. Occitania had not been deeply involved in the Investiture Conflict, when Gregory VII proclaimed the leadership of the Church and demanded the primary allegiance of all Christians. For many men Gregory had posed a hard choice; if they followed him they had to break their oaths to an annointed king. Most of the inhabitants of Occitania did not have to make a choice; they were not closely bound to any secular ruler. They accepted a modicum of reform which neither stimulated their emotions nor changed their habits. Only the First Crusade stirred up some enthusiasm, since count Raymond of Toulouse was one of its principal leaders, but the Occitanians did not develop the same taste for Crusades that the French did. In short, Occitania was a sort of religious backwater, where nothing very exciting had happened for generations and where there had been no occasion to build up zeal for the welfare of the Church and the purity of its doctrine.

In spite of their lack of enthusiasm for the Church, the Occitanians were well aware of religious trends in the rest of Western Europe. And during the twelfth century a wave of popular piety, a desire for a more intense and more personal religious experience, a yearning to bring actual life closer to religious ideals, swept through Europe. This new devotion was best expressed in the life and teaching of St. Bernard of Clairvaux, a neighbor of and a preacher to the Occitanians, but many other religious leaders took part in the movement. Occitania could not be completely untouched by the revival; the Occitanians, like their neighbors, began to search for more satisfactory forms of religious experience. Unfortunately for the future of the country, the most earnest seekers for a new form of religious life had no particular respect for the leaders of the established Church and no strong attachment to orthodox doctrine. Instead, they found greater satisfaction in the teachings of two heretical sects, the Cathars and the Waldensians.

The Cathars were often called Albigensians in the thirteenth century because they were especially numerous in the region of Albi, a town some forty-five miles east of Toulouse. But they were an old and well-established group long before they came to Albi, and the name Cathar expresses one of their basic and enduring beliefs. The "Cathari" were the "purified," those who had broken, as far as possible, their ties to evil, material things. Cathar doctrine was not entirely uniform, but all branches of the sect accepted the idea that the visible world was evil; hence it seems best to describe them by a name that symbolizes their rejection of the world.

Centuries of persecution destroyed almost all Cathar records, though two generations of patient scholarship have begun to recover significant fragments of their writings. We know much more about the Cathars now than we did in 1900, though we are still far from knowing all that we would like to know.

It is certain that the Cathar Church was created by interaction among various heretical sects in the Byzantine Empire. It seems fairly certain that the Cathars were not direct descendants of the Manichaeans, the dualist sect that had so troubled St. Augustine in the fourth century. True dualists assert that there are two equally powerful Gods—an evil God who created the material world and a good God who tries to save man from the evil world. Not all Cathars took this extreme position; many believed that God had permitted Satan to create the world and that in the end God would crush Satan and all his works. Moreover, in recently recovered fragments of Cathar ritual we seem to find traces of very early, pre-Manichaean, almost entirely orthodox Christian rites. Such rituals could have come from churches that became involved in the bitter Christological controversies of the Late Roman Empire—churches that overemphasized the divinity of Christ and denied His humanity, churches that taught that Christ merely took on the appearance of a man and did not really suffer on the cross. Such doctrines, by denying that God ever existed in human, material form, made it easy to believe that matter must be entirely evil. There was also, in completely orthodox writers of the early Church, a puritanical strain, a contempt for the vanities of this world which needed only a little exaggeration to lead to the conclusion that all matter is evil. Views of this sort may have persisted in many parts of Christendom; there is some evidence that there were heretics in Occitania before there was much contact with the heretics of the East.

Whatever the situation in the West, fully developed Cathar doctrine first appeared in the East. Catharism was strongly established in the Balkan peninsula by the year 1000. It struck deep roots in Bosnia, where an organized Cathar Church dominated the country until the fifteenth century. From Bosnia, at the head of the Adriatic, it was easy to send missionaries to northern Italy, and once the belief was established in Italy there was nothing to keep it from spreading to Occitania where it could give form and substance to indigenous heresies.

The Occitanian form of Catharism was probably simpler than the Balkan version as far as doctrine was concerned. It has been well said that many western Cathars seem to have known little about the official doctrine of their Church; they were concerned primarily with the consolation they derived from their religious meetings and with their efforts to maintain high moral standards. But, as far as there was a generally accepted doctrine, it seems to have run something like this. Satan or Lucifer, the highest of the angels, perhaps even a son of God, led by pride and ambition, departed from the realm of pure spirit and created the material world. He made man and woman from clay, but these miserable beings had no soul. According to one version, God took pity on these victims of Satan and gave them souls; another source says that Satan used the souls of the angels who fell with him. In either case the first woman was tempted to commit the sexual act and so the human soul was lost, perpetually imprisoned in the body, which was material and evil. Cathar doctrine on the source of new souls is not clear; some Cathars believed in the transmigration of souls, others that Satan constantly drew on the stock of souls of fallen angels. In any case, sexual intercourse was the greatest sin, for it either condemned an existing soul to another period of imprisonment in matter or it involved a new soul in this evil world.

God again took pity on the wretched human race and sent

his son Jesus to show men how to escape from the power of Satan. Jesus was an emanation from God, but he was not God. Neither was he man; his apparent body was merely an illusion, for pure spirit could have no contact with matter. Thus Jesus did not suffer on the cross and the cross was not to be venerated; it was evil, as all material things were evil; it was a sign of the attempt of Satan to defeat the plans of God. In fact, Satan had failed, but his wicked cunning enabled him to postpone the inevitable, final catastrophe. The saving truths that Jesus had revealed were misinterpreted and falsi-fied, and the orthodox Christian Church was built on these errors. It was a creature of Satan; it worshipped Satan in revering the God of the Old Testament, who was the creator of the material world. Fortunately, the real message of Jesus had been preserved among the Cathars, and more and more people were accepting the truth. The Cathars, the purified, would re-duce their contacts with the material world to an inescapable minimum and so they would be saved. Eventually all souls would be saved and Satan and his world would come to an end. The process would be slow, but on the other hand there was no need for purgatory or for an eternal hell. Purgatory and hell were here on earth; it was punishment enough to have to live in the body, and some souls would have to endure that punishment for many generations.

It is quite possible that no Cathar preacher ever explained his doctrines in exactly the order and with the same emphasis that I have just used. But every one of the ideas mentioned above does appear in one place or another in our records of Cathar beliefs, and the general characteristics of the faith seem fairly certain even if some of the details are unsure. The most striking thing about Cathar doctrine is that much of it could be accepted with very little hesitation by an ordinary, unschooled Catholic layman. He would have heard of the fall of Satan and the other rebellious angels; he would have been taught to fear the power of the devil and the possible presence of the devil in many material objects. He would have been told to despise the pleasures of this world; he would have known that the holiest life was one of extreme asceticism. He would have possessed some vague notion of the doctrine of original sin and he would have realized that the Church considered absolute chastity one of the signs of sanctity. The medieval Church was obsessed by the problem of sex (consider the amount of space given to it in canon law) and for some of its more puritanical members the idea of sexual intercourse was almost as repugnant as it was to the Cathars. Finally, it should be remembered that prospective converts did not hear the whole body of Cathar doctrine expounded all at once. They were much more apt to hear bits and pieces—phrases spoken by friends or brief sermons of wandering preachers. And it was precisely the bits and pieces that were most plausible, most easy to accept. Almost anyone could say: "The world is evil," and yet to say this took one a long way on the road to Catharism.

Moreover, as we shall see, there was almost nothing in

the Cathar ritual to shock an ordinary Catholic. He would hear verse after verse of familiar passages from the New Testament; he would ask forgiveness for his sins; he would repeat the Lord's Prayer. Much was omitted that would have been found in a Catholic Mass, but very little was added that flatly contradicted Catholic teachings. The sermons probably emphasized points of difference more than the ritual, but we know little about the sermons. The few of which we have some record do not try to explain Cathar doctrine in any detail, and consist mainly in quotations from the Scriptures. It would have been very easy to develop a liking for the simplicity and friendliness of Cathar meetings without realizing that one was falling into doctrinal error.

If its doctrine was somewhat involved, the organization of the Cathar Church was simple and uncomplicated. This simplicity gave it a great advantage in its struggle with Catholicism; the Cathars could reach more people with less effort than could their opponents. For example, the Cathars did not need churches; they had "houses," often only large rooms in which the faithful gathered. They had a rudimentary hierarchy; a bishop, assisted by an "elder son" and a "younger son," had general supervision of an area such as the region around Albi, and each community of any size had a deacon. But the work of converting men to the faith and of maintaining their devotion to the faith was chiefly the responsibility of the "perfect." The "perfect" were those who had renounced the world in a solemn public ceremony. They gave up their property; they promised never to eat meat, eggs or any other product of animal intercourse (fish, curiously enough, were permitted); they were never to lie, to take an oath, or to renounce their faith. The "perfect" were the ministers of the Cathar Church; usually they wandered in pairs through the country instead of staying in one place and so were able to keep in close touch with their followers. It is noteworthy that women could be accepted as members of the "perfect," which may help to explain why Catharism was so attractive to many women of Occitania. To be one of the "perfect" gave a woman a higher status in the Cathar Church than she could ever attain in its Catholic rival.

It took relatively little time and almost no money to run such an organization; Cathar leaders could concentrate on their spiritual duties rather than on administrative problems and on long drawn-out lawsuits. Doubtless the Cathars would have had to increase the complexity of their ecclesiastical organization if they had succeeded in establishing themselves as a permanent group in Western society. But the fact that only a small group of extreme ascetics could act as bishops, deacons, and ministers would probably have kept the administrative apparatus from becoming excessively large. In any case, down to the time of its extinction the Cathar hierarchy remained poor, unencumbered by ecclesiastical business or politics, and greatly esteemed by its followers.

The essential acts of Cathar ritual were repeated recitals of the Lord's Prayer, the laying on of hands, and the exchange of the kiss of peace. At an ordinary meeting the faithful simply said the Lord's Prayer, made a general confession of their sins, and asked forgiveness. Often the meeting ended with a common meal. The few accounts we have of these services recall the familial, brotherly atmosphere of early Christian congregations, or of some of the small radical post-Reformation sects.

There were, however, two occasions when a somewhat more elaborate ritual was used. The first was when a man who had shown interest in the faith wanted to become a believer and join the Cathar Church. This ceremony was called the Transmission of the Lord's Prayer. A translation may be found in the Appendix. The essential part of the ritual came when the elder said: "We give you this holy prayer, so that you receive it from God and from us and from the Church and so that you may repeat it at any moment of your life, day and night, alone or in company and so that you must never eat or drink without first saying this prayer."

The second occasion for a formal ceremony came when a believer wanted to become one of the "perfect." The rite was called the Consolation; a translation is given in the Appendix. After taking the vow to abstain from all evil and from all worldly pleasure, the postulant asked pardon for all his sins. The elder then took the Gospels and placed them on the believer's head; the other "perfects" touched him with their right hands, and then they all said: "Our Father, receive thy servant in thy justice and send thy grace and thy Holy Spirit upon him." The service ended with the kiss of peace and with repetitions of the Lord's Prayer.

Very few of those who were attracted by Catharism became one of the "perfect," unless it were on their deathbed, when extreme asceticism no longer posed any problem. (Just so, in the early days of Christianity many converts postponed baptism until the last hour, so that they could die without sin.) But while the number of the "perfect" was small, their influence was enormous. They were called "the good men"; they were sure of a welcome in every town; they were greeted respectfully by most of the people they met. In fact, one of the commonest ways of proving a charge of heresy was to assert that the accused had "adored" one of the "perfect"; that is, that he had asked a blessing. It was this vast army of sympathizers that was the real strength of Catharism, not the relatively small group of the "perfect."

For this mass of sympathizers, Catharism demanded less, in the way of material support and symbolic acts, than did Catholicism. Believers could enjoy the society of the "perfect" without being perfect themselves; they could hope to achieve salvation without repeated acts of penance and reception of the sacraments; they did not have to fear hell or the pains of purgatory. Their enemies, both then and now, have claimed that these aspects of Catharism led to a relaxed morality; that the extreme asceticism of the "perfect" was merely a screen for the voluptuous life of their followers. There is very little evidence to support this contention. Certainly the Cathars did not make saints out of the people of Occitania, but it is equally certain that Cathar leaders prescribed strict moral standards. It is almost impossible to measure degrees of morality but I do not think one could show that strongly Catholic sections of Occitania were any more moral than strongly Cathar sections.

The contrary charge, that Catharism would have extinguished the human race by its denunciation of sexual intercourse, is more logical but almost as lacking in proof. Many religions have extolled absolute chastity with very little effect on overall patterns of reproduction. Relatively few believers in Catharism became members of the "perfect" during the child-producing years. In fact, the population of Occitania grew rapidly during the period of Cathar expansion and declined after Catharism had been extinguished, though religion had little to do with these demographic changes. The spread of Catharism coincided with an economic boom and its fall with a depression and a plague.

The real problem for the Catholic Church was not that Catharism was leading to immorality or race suicide, but that it was interesting a very large part of the population of Occitania and gaining the support of a sizeable minority. Somehow the doctrines and practices of Catharism appealed to the sort of men who would have been reform leaders within the Church in other regions. Somehow Catharism satisfied the religious needs of the sort of people who elsewhere were inspired by a

St. Bernard or a St. Francis. In fair, relatively unhindered competition, Catharism was gaining at the expense of the established church.

The other competitors in the struggle for religious loyalty in Occitania were the Waldensians. Less well organized and much closer in doctrine to Catholicism than the Cathars, the Waldensians of the late twelfth and thirteenth centuries scarcely deserve the name of a church. They thought of themselves as entirely orthodox Catholics, cruelly rebuffed by an organization that they only sought to purify and to reform. It was only after repeated disappointments and persecutions that the Waldensians finally gave up the attempt to demonstrate their orthodoxy and formed the separatist Waldensian Church that endures to this day.

The Waldensians were founded by Peter Waldo of Lyons in 1160 but it was only in the 1180's that they began to worry the Catholic Church. Waldo at first seemed only a guilt-stricken rich man, like many others, who wished to atone for his sins by giving away his wealth and by doing good works. When he formed a small fraternity of other like-minded men he was still doing nothing more than other pious laymen had done. But it gradually became apparent that Waldo was interested more in reform than in charity, was concerned more with saving souls than bodies. His "Poor Men of Lyons" began to preach, trying to turn their fellow-citizens away from their vanities, and also blaming the ordained clergy for their wealth and their indifference to the spiritual needs of the people. It was this tendency to attack the priesthood that eventually turned the Church against Waldo. In many ways he was only trying to do what St. Francis of Assisi did a generation later—to reach discouraged laymen by living among them, and to make the sermon instead of the ceremony the central religious experience. But Waldo stubbornly rejected the discipline of the Church while St. Francis accepted the rulings of higher authority without question. And St. Francis had the good fortune of dealing with Pope Innocent III while Waldo had to negotiate with more timid and less imaginative pontiffs. When Waldo was ordered to stop preaching he refused to obey, and made his disobedience a basic article of his reform movement. With the help of some telling examples from the history of the early Church, he argued that all true Christians could preach the Gospel. Even worse, from the viewpoint of the twelfth century, he saw no reason why women should not be allowed to preach as well as men. (Here again we find that unusual acceptance of the equality of women that seems to have had an especial appeal to the ladies of Occitania.) Waldo had been driven to deny any basic distinction between layman and cleric.

Such a doctrine obviously attacked the validity of ordination, the authority of the Church, and the significance of the apostolic succession. By implication it weakened the value of the sacraments, since, in case of necessity, they could be administered by laymen. But Waldo and his followers were rebelling against the organization of the Church, not its doctrine.

As far as possible, they adhered to a strictly orthodox theology; they were as shocked by the teachings of the Cathars as any Catholic. These "unlearned laymen," as their opponents called them, doubtless fell into some errors on subtle theological questions, but on all essential points—the value of the Old Testament, the Trinity, the Incarnation, the Redemption—they were in complete agreement with the Catholics and violently opposed to the Cathars. They were very like a moderate Protestant sect of the sixteenth century; they rejected the headship of the pope and the special status of the clergy, but they accepted all essential Christian doctrines.

Nevertheless, Cathars and Waldensians were sometimes confused with each other in Occitania, and it seems likely that there was some mingling of the two beliefs among the more ignorant part of the population. After all, the two groups resembled each other in some ways. Their leaders preached and practiced absolute poverty; they traveled incessantly through the land on their missionary efforts; they rejected the authority of the established Church. For men who were not capable of understanding anything but the crudest elements of doctrine—and this must have been a large group—the essence of the new sects must have seemed to be scorn of worldly goods, intimate contact with the masses, and rebellion against the Roman Church. On these three points Cathars and Waldensians agreed.

The Waldensians entered Occitania much later than the Cathars and while they spread throughout the country they were neither as numerous nor as influential as their rivals. If the only heretics in Occitania had been Waldensians, the popes would not have taken the extreme measures they did. The real enemy of the Catholic Church was the Cathar Church. In attacking the Cathars it was easy enough to catch most of the Waldensians as well, but they were not the main target. The Cathar Church was annihilated; the Waldensian Church was savagely persecuted, but a fraction of it survived.

III

THE CHURCH
COUNTERATTACKS

If the prelates of Occitania were unconcerned about the spread
of heresy, the leaders of the Roman Church were not. As early
as 1145 St. Bernard of Clairvaux led a mission to Occitania to
warn the faithful against the dangers of heresy and to recon-
vert those who had fallen into error. St. Bernard was the un-
official head of the Western Church and the most eloquent
preacher of his day. Yet this man, who could make popes and
determine the decisions of kings, had very little success in
Occitania. He drew crowds, as he did everywhere, but if the
Occitanians enjoyed his eloquence they were not convinced by
his arguments. St. Bernard himself was discouraged; he painted
a black picture of a land where the churches were empty and
where heresy was triumphant. St. Bernard was apt to exag-
gerate, but even if we give full allowance for his love of decla-
mation, it still is clear that there were a great many heretics
in the country.

For the next sixty years the Church carried on a patient—

and futile—argument with the heretics. Missions were sent, headed by able and eloquent men; none of them had any real impact on the people of Occitania. Thus in 1178 a papal legate secured the condemnation of Pierre Maurand, a rich merchant of Toulouse, who was certainly friendly with heretics and who was probably a convert to Catharism. Pierre abjured his heretical beliefs and was sentenced to spend three years as a penitent in the Holy Land. When he returned, the citizens of Toulouse elected him as one of their consuls—that is, a member of the governing body of the city. It is not surprising that few other heretics felt it necessary to renounce their faith.

The last and greatest missionary effort came just before the Church turned, in despair and in anger, to the use of force. In 1203 Pierre de Castelnau, a Cistercian monk, was sent as legate to the infected area. He had another Cistercian as companion; soon they were joined by Arnaud Amaury, abbot of Cîteaux and head of their order. The Cistercians no longer held the preeminent position in the Church that they had enjoyed in the time of St. Bernard, but they were still an elite group, famous for their discipline, their piety, and their asceticism. They were the best that the Church had to use against the heretics, but the best was not good enough; the mission accomplished very little. In 1205 the Cistercian mission was joined by two Spaniards, the bishop of Osma and his subprior, Dominic de Guzman. It was a symbolic meeting; the head of the last of the great medieval reforming monastic congregations was handing on the torch of religious leadership to the

41

founder of the first of the new reforming orders of friars. St. Dominic already saw the value of the ideal of absolute poverty; if he and his fellows would wander, barefoot and penniless, through the country, they might gain the same veneration that was given to Cathar leaders. The new technique was successful up to a point; the missionaries were treated with greater respect than before and they were given a fair chance to explain their views. There were several formal debates in which Catholic and Cathar leaders discussed the differences between their beliefs, but, as usually happens in such cases, very few of the listeners changed their minds. Nothing reveals more clearly the climate of opinion in Occitania than the fact that heretics could discuss their doctrines publicly and argue as equals with the representatives of the pope. Nothing angered the missionaries more than the necessity of engaging in these long and fruitless debates. Even St. Dominic is said to have lost his temper on one occasion and to have threatened the use of force. In any case, the great missionary effort of 1203–1207 was a failure. Few heretics were converted, and the people of Occitania continued to tolerate and even to admire the Cathars.

Even before the failure of missionary endeavor was apparent, there had been suggestions that heresy could be wiped out only by the use of armed force. Alexander III (1159–1181) had considered the idea of asking pious secular princes to attack the heretics, but in the one document in which he actually called for military operations he lumped the Cathars with mercenaries, bandits, and other undesirables, and thus confused the idea of protecting the faith with the idea of preserving public order. The one result of his exhortation was an attack in 1181 on the heretical town of Lavaur, an attack organized by his legate (also a Cistercian abbot) and supported by Catholic nobles of the region. The siege was successful, but it was not followed up, and it scarcely slowed the growth of heresy. The fact that Lavaur was a Trencavel town, and that the Trencavels had many enemies probably had as much to do with the legate's victory as any zeal for Catholicism.

The popes of the twelfth century, in spite of all their troubles with rebellious Romans and overbearing emperors, were not eager to take up arms against their enemies. Often, in St. Bernard's words, they found it wiser to "exchange the City for the world"; that is, to flee Rome, take refuge in France, and wait for time to destroy their enemies. When they found it impossible to avoid warfare, they limited the conflict as far as they could and did not try to turn a defense of Rome or the Papal States into a Crusade. Alexander III, who had more reason than many popes to hate the emperor and his Italian allies, never proclaimed a Crusade against Frederick Barbarossa, which may be one reason why he was only half-hearted in urging a Crusade against the Cathars. But, beginning with Innocent III (1198–1216) and continuing throughout the thirteenth century, the popes showed themselves more and more willing to use Crusades as a way of raising armies against heretics and disobedient Christians. This easy resort to force, this sanctification of violence by promises of remission of sins, proved to be one of the worst mistakes in the history of the papacy. A series of impressive victories led to an even more impressive series of catastrophies. By using the Crusade to crush the Hohenstaufen rulers of Germany and southern Italy, the popes created the Italian anarchy that forced them to take refuge in Avignon and the German anarchy that made possible the Reformation. By using the French as the chief components of their crusading armies, the popes built up the power of the French king and created the dependence on France that led to the humiliation of Boniface VIII, the capitulation of Clement V, the Babylonian Captivity, and the Great Schism. The Crusades against the heretics of Occitania—the Albigensian Crusades—were the first large-scale use of this new and dangerous technique of using the Holy War to attain the objectives of the papacy in Europe.

Innocent III's decision to proclaim a Crusade against the heretics was fateful, but it was not the result of a sudden, foolish impulse. Innocent was a reasonable man and a patient man—up to certain limits. He would negotiate as long as he saw hope in negotiation; he would procrastinate as long as he thought time was on his side; but he would not accept defeat or even a prolonged postponement of victory. Other popes were willing to start controversies that could be settled only by their successors; they would accept temporary setbacks in their confidence that the eternal and unforgetting Church would eventually gain its case. Innocent was determined to finish what he started; he did not want to be vindicated by posterity. The pattern was repeated again and again in his pontificate—years of investigation and discussion followed by sharp, brutal decisions. A man of this temperament sooner or later was going to use force.

Innocent's tendency to rely, in the end, on force, was surely encouraged by his knowledge that force was easily available. The century that ran from 1185 to 1285 was the great century of the Crusades. Almost every year during that century a Crusade was being planned or was actually being waged. It was the century of the Third Crusade (1189–1193) the Fourth and Fifth Crusades (1202–1204, 1217–1221), the Crusades of Frederick II (1228), of Thibaud of Champagne (1239–1241), and of St. Louis (1248–1254, 1270) to mention only the major overseas expeditions. It was also the century of the Albigensian Crusades (1209–1226) and of the Crusades against the Hohenstaufen (which filled most of the years between 1240 and 1268). It was the century that ended with the Crusade against Aragon (1285), the expedition that finally convinced the French, who formed the backbone of most crusading armies, that Crusades were futile and that papal policy was mistaken.

But before that final disillusionment, every young man of good family, and especially every young Frenchman of good family, felt the urge to go on a Crusade. Crusading satisfied all the aspirations of the military class—the desire to show one's skill and courage in armed combat, the desire to gain fame among one's peers, the desire to serve God and the

Church. Not everyone who took crusading vows fulfilled them, and many of those who did fulfill them did so in a perfunctory way—one skirmish with Saracen or heretic was enough to satisfy honor. But a surprisingly large number of men did take the Crusades seriously; they spent years away from home and risked their lives in forays, sieges, and battles. There were families which generation after generation sent their sons to the Crusades—not least the royal family of France. Five French kings in succession led Crusades (Louis VII, Philip Augustus, Louis VIII, Louis IX, and Philip III). Of these five kings, the last three died on Crusade. With this example to inspire them, it is not surprising that the French were the most zealous crusaders, and that an appeal to the French by a pope seldom went unheeded.

Innocent could have had no doubts about French willingness to engage in Crusades overseas. But an experiment early in his pontificate proved that they also could be enticed into fighting for the Church in Europe. The sudden and unexpected deaths of Constance, Queen of Sicily and of her husband, the emperor Henry VI, had left a three-year-old boy, Frederick II, as heir of the kingdom of Sicily. Naturally, there were squabbles over the regency; equally naturally, Innocent III was determined to have the final word in settling the disputes. After all, Sicily was a fief of the papacy and the Papal States were not safe if Sicily was in unfriendly hands. Unfortunately for the papacy, a very unfriendly German, Markward of Anweiler, was gaining a strong position in Sicily. Markward had been one of Henry VI's ablest generals and administrators; he symbolized the German attempt to dominate Italy that Innocent felt must be repelled at all costs. In 1199 Innocent proclaimed a Crusade against Markward, and gave full crusading privileges to a group of Frenchmen who fought against him. This tiny Crusade was at least partially successful; the growth of Markward's power was checked and no one was able to take his place when he died in 1202. Innocent should have been pleased with the results; he had thwarted a dangerous enemy with minimum risks and costs, and he had found that French nobles would support him even if their king took little interest in the conflict.

These things must have been in Innocent's mind as he looked at the situation in Occitania in 1207. Preaching, argument, and exhortation had accomplished almost nothing. The natural leaders of the country, the counts of Toulouse and Foix, the Trencavel viscounts, the lesser lords, and the town governments were unable and unwilling to take any decisive steps against heresy. They could not trust their own subordinates: The seneschal of the viscount of Béziers and Albi was a heretic. They did not wish to harm their relatives and friends: The sister of the count of Foix had become one of the "perfect"; there were almost certainly Cathars in the household of the count of Toulouse. To root out heresy would have required a civil war and there were already enough smoldering quarrels in the country to discourage the starting of a new set of feuds. Raymond VI of Toulouse set the example for

most of the other barons of Occitania: He answered politely
when he was asked to crush the heretics; he insisted that he
was a pious and orthodox Catholic; and he did nothing.
Spiritual persuasion and ecclesiastical sanctions had failed;
appeals to the princes of the land had failed; the heretics were
setting up a rival church. Innocent III was not a man to accept
a stalemate; if peaceful measures were unsuccessful then force
must be used.

Innocent had begun to threaten the heretics with invasion
even before the failure of his missionaries was evident. In 1204
and 1205 he asked Philip Augustus of France to help him suppress heresy; in 1207 he urged Philip to put himself at the
head of a full-fledged Crusade against the Cathars of Occitania.
The pope suggested that the crusaders would receive more than
spiritual benefits; they could seize the lands of southern lords
who had protected or tolerated heresy. This doctrine of "ex-
position to prey" did not altogether please the French king.
According to his ideas, if a lord were a heretic or a protector of
heretics, his lands should be forfeited to his feudal superior,
not to any chance adventurer who was able to seize them. In
the end, Philip's doctrine prevailed, but he had some anxious
moments when it seemed as if his nominal suzerainty over parts
of Occitania were going to be ignored. Meanwhile, he had an
excellent excuse for avoiding involvements in the South. He
had just conquered Normandy and Anjou from John of England, but he was by no means sure that he could hold these
provinces. He asked Innocent to arrange a truce between

France and England and to guarantee that John would not attack if the royal army moved south. Innocent naturally could not give such promises—no one could ever guarantee what John of England would do—and so Philip Augustus remained aloof from the first of the Albigensian Crusades.

Nevertheless, the fact that the pope asked help from the king of France and his vassals is significant. In spite of many quarrels, the French royal house had been a more consistent supporter of the papacy than any other ruling family. In spite of broken vows and token service, the French nobility had furnished more soldiers for Crusades than the feudal class of any other country. Innocent felt that he could trust the French to respect the rights of the Church even while they gained lands and income for themselves. He could not trust any other people. Catharism was as rife in northern Italy as it was in Occitania, but if Innocent had preached a Crusade against the Italian heretics, he would have had to call in the Germans. Such an act would have destroyed the liberties of the Italian cities, who were strong supporters of the papacy, and would have strengthened the emperor, who posed the greatest threat to papal independence. Therefore in Italy Innocent, much against his instincts, had to temporize, and leave the solution of the problem of heresy to his successors. The fact that Catharism in Italy was finally eliminated by more or less peaceful means makes one wonder if the Albigensian Crusades were really necessary. Even in Occitania, the religious revival inspired by the mendicant orders and the legal processes of the Inquisition did more to destroy heresy than the Crusades. In Italy the mendicants, their allies among the secular clergy, and the inquisitors did the whole job, without calling in foreign conquerors. The patient Innocent III was a little too impatient in dealing with Occitania.

Almost all scholars are agreed that Innocent III would have eventually proclaimed a Crusade against the heretics, but an act of political folly gave him an excuse for acting sooner rather than later. In 1207 the legate Pierre de Castelnau had excommunicated Raymond VI of Toulouse and had placed his lands under an interdict. Pierre had several reasons for this action. Raymond, like many other feudal lords, had quarreled with and dispossessed prelates of the Church, and his mercenaries were almost as cruel and destructive as those of John of England or Philip Augustus of France. But the real grievance against Raymond was that he was protecting heretics and making no effort to expel them from his lands. Innocent had confirmed Pierre's action in a bitter letter of 29 May, 1207, in which he threatened to call in other princes to cleanse the count's lands from the infection of heresy. Raymond must have known that his situation was precarious, for Innocent followed up his denunciation with his appeal to Philip Augustus and with letters to the barons and knights of France urging them to make war on the heretics of the South. But it is doubtful whether Raymond realized the full extent of his danger. It was not particularly shocking to be excommunicated; almost every European ruler, including John and Philip Augustus, was at one time or another under the ban of the Church. Excommunication usually led to long negotiations which ended in a formal submission to the Church and a compromise on the real points at issue. Raymond tried to play the game according to the usual formula; what he failed to realize was that Innocent was in no mood to compromise. In two conferences with the papal legates Raymond refused to make any real concessions; he would promise anything but he would do nothing. The second conference, in January 1208, broke up in a wrangle; according to Innocent III, Raymond warned the legates that he would keep an eye on them wherever they went. The next day, 14 January, the legate Pierre de Castelnau was assassinated as he was preparing to cross the Rhône. The assassin was almost certainly a native of the country; it is almost equally certain that he acted without the knowledge of Raymond VI. Raymond was not a political genius, but he certainly had sense enough to know that the assassination of a papal legate was a sure road to ruin. The fact that the name of the assassin was never discovered is another indication of Raymond's innocence; a member of the count's household, a man bound to him in any way, would surely have been recognized. In the end, even Innocent admitted that there was no real proof, but only suspicion of complicity against Raymond. Raymond can justly be blamed for helping to create the atmosphere that made the murder possible, but so can Pierre de Castelnau. The legate was not an easygoing man and he had many enemies besides the count. In fact, it is somewhat surprising that in a land of violence and personal feuds he had not been assassinated before the second conference.

It is, of course, futile to argue about Raymond's guilt or innocence. The important thing was the opinion of contemporaries, and they believed, almost unanimously, that Raymond was guilty. On 10 March, Innocent wrote again to Philip Augustus and to the clergy and people of France denouncing Raymond, renewing his appeal for a Crusade against the heretics, and offering the lands of the count of Toulouse and other supporters of heresy to those who could conquer them. Philip Augustus, as cautious as ever, still refused to move, and reminded the pope rather sharply that the Holy See had no right to dispose of fiefs held of the king of France. But the French nobility was at last aroused. We do not have to believe the report of the papal legates that the crusading army was the largest ever seen in Christendom; they had no means of knowing the size of either their own or any earlier forces. But Philip Augustus felt it necessary to try to limit the number of men joining the Crusade—the duke of Burgundy and the count of Nevers were to take only five hundred knights in their contingent and all five hundred were to come from Burgundy. Five hundred was certainly more than half the number of men of knightly rank in Burgundy; even if Nevers furnished a few score, almost every young man connected with a knightly family must have enlisted. Granting that Burgundy and Nevers were close neighbors of Occitania, and that the longer the journey to the scene of conflict the less the response, it still seems that many thousands of Frenchmen must have taken the Cross. Never was a Crusade so attractive, never were crusading vows easier to fulfill. The cause seemed just and the rewards were great. Remission of sins was certain and the Crusade could take the place of all other penance. The chances for plunder were good and the acquisition of new lands was possible. Best of all, a crusader had to serve only forty days to secure all the indulgences granted to participants in the Holy War. This forty-day rule is one reason why no one can estimate the size of the crusading army; it was constantly increasing and diminishing as contingents came and left. But it also made it easy to prolong the Crusade for many years, since fresh forces were always available. As young men came of age, as older men thought more about their sins, new waves of crusaders poured down from the North. The journey was easy, inexpensive, and safe, compared with the hazards of a voyage to the Holy Land. As in all wars, really bloody conflicts were rare; a man might serve his forty days without doing anything more strenuous than riding through a few villages to overawe the inhabitants. The really surprising thing is that the crusading army was no larger, that there were barons and knights who never took part in the expedition.

The one handicap of the crusaders was their lack of organization. The nominal leader was the papal legate, Arnaud Amaury of Cîteaux, but the legate, for all his political skill, could scarcely command an army. The highest-ranking laymen were the duke of Burgundy, and the counts of Nevers, St. Pol, and Boulogne. None of these men wanted to spend years in the South; none of them had the tenacity or the military skill that were going to be needed if the Crusade became a real war instead of a military demonstration. It took some months for the legate to realize that among the minor barons there was a remarkable leader, Simon, lord of Montfort.[1] By the time that Simon had been recognized as commander-in-chief and secular head of the Crusade, the summer soldiers had gone home and the crusading army had been reduced to a fraction of its original size. Simon was a good field commander, but his greatest quality was his ability to build an effective army out of shifting groups of men from all parts of France, and, in a pinch, out of mercenaries of dubious reputation and doubtful reliability. Without Simon, the poor organization and fluctuating composition of the crusading army would have led almost certainly to an early collapse of the expedition. Even with Simon, it proved impossible to keep a large enough army together long enough to ensure a complete victory.

---

[1] Simon was also earl of Leicester in England, an honor he had inherited through his mother. John recognized Simon's title, but as long as John and Philip Augustus were at war the earldom was of little value to Simon. He had to fight the war largely with the resources of his French fief.

IV

THE FIRST CAMPAIGN —BÉZIERS AND CARCASSONNE

If lack of unity was a handicap for the French, it was a disaster for the Occitanians. A united South could perhaps have negotiated a settlement with the crusaders that would have avoided serious war at the cost of wiping out a few notorious groups of heretics. Failing this, a united South could have made the war so costly that ideas of conquest would have had to be abandoned. But the lords of Occitania could not agree on any policy, especially during the crucial first two years.

The lack of unity was rooted in the history of the country; it was not caused by differences in religion. Very few of the Catholics of Occitania favored the Crusade. Some, as we shall see, took the Cross for purely political reasons, but really convinced, fighting crusaders came mainly from the fringes of the country. An army of Occitanians was raised in the northwest, a region that was already somewhat Francicized; it captured a few strongholds in Quercy, but took no part in the main action. Some lords from Provence joined the principal army, but they became disillusioned when they found the Crusade changing from a punitive expedition into a war of conquest by the French. Otherwise, opinion was almost unanimous; heretics might be bad, but northerners were worse. The problem was to find a way of getting the northerners out of the country, and here was where all the old jealousies and suspicions did their damage. Especially dangerous was the old rivalry between the count of Toulouse and his nominal vassal, the Trencavel viscount of Béziers; each feared that the other might try to use the Crusade to break his power, and each may have been right. The count of Foix was a more reliable supporter of the count of Toulouse, but Raymond Roger of Foix was all fighter and no politician, while Raymond VI of Toulouse was not much of a fighter and perhaps a little too complacent about his political skill. And if the greatest lords of the South seldom agreed, there was no more harmony among the lesser men.

Raymond of Toulouse had a plan that might have just barely worked; it was to bow to the storm, join the Crusade, persecute enough heretics to satisfy the Church that local leaders could protect the faith, and thus remove all reason for outside intervention. The scheme was ingenious; one of the benefits of taking the Cross was that all the possessions of a crusader were placed under the protection of the Church. If all the lords of Occitania joined the Crusade there would be nothing to attack, nothing to confiscate, and the northerners would have to go home.

The trouble was that the plan was a little too ingenious;

it assumed that the Church would accept the promises of men who had already promised much and delivered little, and it also assumed that lords who did not really want to destroy a considerable number of their subjects would suddenly become active persecutors of heretics. Raymond was to find that neither of these assumptions was sound. If he had had to deal with Innocent III his scheme might have worked, at least for a few years, for Innocent showed some understanding of Raymond's difficult situation and some regard for Raymond's rights. But Innocent was under terrific pressure from his legates, men who had become convinced that no Occitanian baron could ever be trusted. They had been disappointed and deceived too many times; they could not be satisfied by any promises or pledges that Raymond gave; they could never be convinced that Raymond really meant to attack heresy. This time they were going to finish the job. Arnaud Amaury, in particular, was implacable, and as long as he was the pope's chief adviser on the problem of heresy, Raymond had no real chance of reaching a reasonable agreement with the Church.

In 1209, however, Raymond did not realize how great was the hostility against him. He tried in vain to reach an agreement with Raymond Roger Trencavel, viscount of Béziers, for common defense action; when the viscount repulsed him he decided to act alone. If he could be reconciled to the Church, his lands, at least, would be spared. Raymond knew that Arnaud Amaury had no confidence in him, but perhaps another legate would be more accommodating. So the count asked Innocent III to send a new legate, promising to accept all the demands of the Church.

Innocent handled the count's request adroitly, perhaps a little too adroitly to save his reputation for complete honesty. He sent his secretary, Milo, as legate, but ordered Milo to obey Arnaud Amaury in all things. He also suggested that it did not really matter whether the count was sincere or not. If Raymond did mean to keep his promises, then some of the largest groups of heretics would be left without a protector. If Raymond was not sincere, there was still much to be gained by accepting a feigned submission. Raymond could not resist the Crusade while trying to persuade the pope that he was a reformed character, and if Raymond did not resist, lesser lords could be easily crushed. Then, with all possible allies swept away, Raymond in his turn could be overwhelmed. That Innocent was actually thinking in these terms is proved by his letter to his legates. "You ask us urgently what policy the crusaders should adopt with respect to the count of Toulouse. Follow the advice of the apostle who said: 'I was clever, I took you by tricking you.' After talking things over with the most sensible leaders of the army you should attack those who have destroyed the unity of the Church one after the other, so that their forces will be divided. Don't begin by attacking the count, if you see that he is not rushing foolishly to defend the others. Be wise and conceal your intentions; leave him alone at first in order to attack those who are openly rebellious. It will not be easy to crush the adherents of Antichrist if we let them unite for a common defense. On the other hand, nothing will be easier than to crush them, if the count does not aid them. Perhaps the sight of their disaster will really reform him. But if he persists in his evil plans, when he is isolated and supported only by his own forces, we can defeat him without too much trouble."

It is only fair to say that Raymond may have had some devious plans of his own. The evidence for that is not as good as it is for Innocent's scheming, but Raymond could have hoped that the Crusade would weaken his unruly vassals, especially the viscount of Béziers, and thus strengthen his position. After all, few Crusades had been able to mount more than one or two effective offensives; after the first real success most of the army returned home. Raymond Roger of Béziers should have been able to hold out for a year or more; if he were defeated only after a long and difficult campaign, there would probably be little enthusiasm left for continuing the Crusade. The French would leave the country, and Raymond of Toulouse could pick up the pieces of the Trencavel principality.

Whatever his reasons, Raymond was determined to reconcile himself with the Church, whatever the cost. He admitted all his faults, ranging from his failure to observe solemn feast days to his protection of heretics; he promised to correct his errors; and as a pledge for good behavior he placed seven of his castles in the hands of the Church. On 18 June, 1209, he repeated these promises in public, was scourged by the legate Milo, and was restored to the communion of the Church. The next day he took the Cross and promised to aid the leaders of the crusading army in every way. If a policy of appeasement could have saved him, Raymond had done all that anyone could have asked.

Meanwhile the crusading army had started its march south. It left Lyons on 24 June, and had arrived at Montpellier, one of the few thoroughly Catholic cities of the South, by 20 July. The submission of the count of Toulouse had changed the military objectives of the Crusade; the target was now the lands of the viscount of Béziers rather than Raymond's principality. Raymond Roger of Béziers had at least as bad a reputation for tolerating heretics as Raymond of Toulouse, and his strongholds dominated the region where the Cathars were most numerous. He was the logical man to attack; the only problem was that his strongholds were really strong. One of the basic rules of medieval warfare was never to risk a pitched battle with an invading army while it was fresh and full of enthusiasm. Men who broke this rule, as Harold of England did at Hastings, were running unnecessary and often disastrous risks. The prudent course was to retire before the enemy, concentrate defense forces in a few strongly fortified positions, and wait for the tedium of siege warfare, the inevitable diseases of camp life, and the probable shortage of supplies to weaken the invader. The obvious counterstrategy was for the attacker to seek a quick victory in the field, or, if faced with a siege, to seize every opportunity, no matter how risky, to penetrate the enemy fortress.

The campaign of 1209 offers a classic example of the application of these rules. Raymond Roger did not have much space for maneuver, but he retired to Carcassonne, the most remote and most strongly fortified of his towns. Between Carcassonne and the crusaders lay Béziers, also strongly fortified and well garrisoned. The burghers of Béziers were not entirely happy at being deserted by their viscount, but they were quite confident that they could resist any siege. They were a tough lot; they had assassinated viscount Raymond I in 1167, they had the usual contempt of Occitanians for the clergy, and they had been practically autonomous for many years. They showed their confidence when their bishop, Renaud de Montpeyroux, asked them to turn over 222 heretics to ensure the safety of the city. We have the list of names that he gave, which seems to have included only heads of families, or perhaps only the leaders of the heretics, for Renaud suggested that if the Catholic citizens felt it unsafe to act, they could leave the town and escape the punishment that would be inflicted on the guilty. Some two hundred heretics would not have been enough to terrorize a city of eight to ten thousand people; there must have been many more followers of the two proscribed religions (for Waldensians appeared on the list) and at least an equal number of sympathizers. Whatever the actual figures, the citizens of Béziers refused flatly to betray their unorthodox brethren. As was to be shown again and again during the following decades, the Occitanians felt that the argument between Catholic and heretic was their own private affair, and that the real enemy was the French intruder.

With ordinary prudence, the confidence of the men of Béziers in their ability to resist the crusading army would not have been misplaced. It was almost impossible to storm a fortified town, and if the siege had lasted more than a few weeks the great majority of the crusaders would have fulfilled their obligations and gone home. All that was needed was to sit tight and not provoke the enemy. Instead, the day the siege began (22 July) some of the burghers made a rash and unorganized sortie. In the confused fighting that followed, the defenders were forced back to their gates and the crusaders were able to enter the city along with their fleeing enemies. Once the attackers were inside the walls the gates could not be closed, and more and more men poured in.

There followed one of the most pitiless massacres of the Middle Ages. No one was spared, Catholics and heretics, men and women, clerics and children were all put to the sword. It is not true that the leaders of the Crusade shouted: "Kill them all; God will know his own!" But the German monk who invented this story a few years later accurately reported the mood of the crusading army. In reporting the victory to the pope, the legate Arnaud Amaury said cheerfully that neither age nor sex was spared and that about twenty thousand people were killed. The figure is certainly too high; the striking point is that the legate expressed no regret about the massacre, not even a word of condolence for the clergy of the cathedral who were killed in front of their own altar.

A southern, but Catholic chronicler of the Crusade believed that the massacre was a deliberate act of policy. He says that the leaders had agreed "that in any fortified place that would not surrender, all the inhabitants were to be killed when the place was taken. Then they would find no one to resist them. . . . This is why Béziers was ruined and destroyed, why its inhabitants were slain. All were killed, even those who took refuge in the church. Nothing could save them, neither crucifix nor altar. Women and children were killed, the clergy were killed by those crazy, damnable foot-soldiers. No one escaped; may God, if He will, receive their souls in Paradise. I do not believe that such an enormous and savage massacre ever took place before, even in the time of the Saracens."

It is true that most of the fighting and most of the killing was done by foot-soldiers, camp-followers, and mercenaries. These men were the least disciplined and most brutal element in the crusading army. The mounted men, knights, squires, and barons were the last to enter the city. But this supposedly more chivalrous group of crusaders made no effort to stop the atrocities that were being committed before their eyes. Their indignation was aroused only when the foot-soldiers started looting. This was an infringement on the perquisites of the upper classes and was promptly and swiftly repressed. But if the nobles could stop looting they could have stopped the killing. It is hard not to believe that the massacre was a deliberate act of terror and that the legate was responsible for it. At the very least, he had created an atmosphere of hatred for heretics and their friends which made it easy for the contagion of slaughter to spread.

Deliberate or not, the massacre of Béziers gave the Crusade the quick, initial success that it needed, and broke the resistance of most of the Trencavel lands. The army rested three days in the fields outside Béziers, sharing the booty among the nobles and preparing for the march on Carcassonne. Then the advance began, slowed by the lords who rode in to make their submission and gain the protection of the Church. The great city of Narbonne promised to (and did) take severe measures against its heretics, and dozens of lords surrendered their castles to the army. Others simply abandoned their lands and took refuge in the mountains. The crusaders spent six days in marching the forty-five miles from Béziers to Carcassonne, but it was time well spent. The army now had a solid, well-provisioned base area in the heart of enemy territory.

The city of Carcassonne was not quite as well fortified in the thirteenth century as it was in the nineteenth (thanks to the efforts of that ferocious restorer Viollet-le-Duc), but it was, nevertheless, almost impregnable. Perched on top of a steep hill, surrounded by massive walls, with no cover for the assailants outside the walls, there could be no thought of taking the city by storm. The crusaders settled down to a regular siege, and what should have been a long one. But the siege took place during the warmest part of the summer and Carcassonne, on its hill, began to run short of water. The two suburbs of the city had been taken after hard fighting; refugees from these outposts, added to those who had already fled to Carcassonne as the crusading army advanced, must have terribly overcrowded the city. If viscount Raymond Roger had been able to hold out until fall, it is likely that the besieging army would have melted away, but apparently Raymond Roger feared that prolonged resistance was becoming impossible. He tried to get one of his suzerains, the strictly Catholic king of Aragon, to intercede for him, but Peter of Aragon could secure only a promise that the viscount and twelve of his followers could depart in peace. This was small consolation to a man who knew the fate of Béziers and Raymond Roger decided to act for himself. There are various stories as to the terms on which he entered the crusaders' camp. He must have had some kind of a safe conduct or he could not have negotiated at all; on the other hand, he was treated as a prisoner of war and remained in captivity until his death a few months later.

In any case, Raymond Roger and the men who held the city in his name were able to spare Carcassonne the fate of Béziers. According to the terms of the capitulation, all the inhabitants had to depart; all their property, down to the last penny, was seized as booty; but there was to be no killing. Even the heretics—and there were some notorious Cathar leaders in the city—were allowed to depart in peace. The plundering was systematic and orderly; no houses were destroyed, and many of the Catholic citizens eventually returned and took up their former occupations.

The contrast between the massacre of Béziers and the businesslike occupation of Carcassonne is striking, especially when one remembers that the two events were separated by less than a month. Certainly the crusaders made more of a profit out of the thorough and well-organized confiscation of the goods of the people of Carcassonne than they had out of the wild, unsystematic looting of Béziers. Certainly it must have occurred to some leaders that ruined towns without inhabitants were not a good foundation on which to build new lordships. Certainly the treatment of Carcassonne shows that it was possible to discipline a crusading army and thus strengthens the hypothesis that the massacre at Béziers was a deliberate act of terror. But the essential difference was that Raymond Roger was not at Béziers, and that he was at Carcassonne. He was the lord of the region the Crusade was trying to conquer; he was the archetype of the Occitanian prince who was technically a Catholic but who actually protected and encouraged heresy. Once Raymond Roger had surrendered to the crusaders, he could be made an object lesson to all his fellow-rulers. His lands could be granted to a true Catholic (that is, a Frenchman), and he could be held as a prisoner until death. The crusaders might kill thousands of heretics, but heresy could not be wiped out until the lords of Occitania either moved wholeheartedly to suppress the disease or else were replaced. The calculation was cold and exact; it was worth letting some thousands of heretics go free if Raymond Roger could be kept in prison.

The evidence for this assertion is provided by the events that followed the fall of Carcassonne. The first thought of the legate was to find a new, trustworthy, Catholic viscount of Béziers and Carcassonne. The principality was offered in turn to the duke of Burgundy and the counts of Nevers and St. Pol— probably out of pure politeness, since each of them had all he could do to rule his own lands. It is also likely, though it cannot be proved, that Philip Augustus was opposed to allowing one of his great barons to increase his strength so markedly; after all, it was the accumulation of several large fiefs in the hands of one man that had made the Plantagenets such deadly enemies of the Capetians. In any case, the great lords declined the honor, and, after some discussion, the choice fell on Simon de Montfort. Simon was not powerful enough in France to cause any jealousy, and he had already shown that he possessed two qualities that were essential for a leader of the Crusade, bravery and loyalty to the Church. During the strangely perverted Fourth Crusade, Simon had been one of the few crusaders who had refused to attack the Christian city of Zara; instead, following papal orders, he had gone to the Holy Land. He had fought well there. And he had distinguished himself during the siege of Carcassonne. He was, as it turned out, exactly the right man to finish the job.

Simon was surely ambitious, but he was also realistic. He

knew that the bulk of the crusading army would soon go home; he knew that while he had a solid base in the Béziers-Carcassonne area, much of the Trencavel lands remained to be conquered. He also knew that his title was uncertain; how could the Church confer a lordship on a complete stranger unless the overlords of the district accepted the fact. It is not surprising that Simon hesitated, and that he made the leaders of the Crusade swear to come to his aid if he fell into difficulties. But in the end he accepted the burden. As he had foreseen, the army dwindled steadily. The count of Nevers departed; after a futile assault on Cabaret, the duke of Burgundy also took the homeward route. Simon was left with some thirty knights and a handful of mercenaries to hold a half-conquered country.

The winter of 1209-1210 began well and ended badly for Simon. Limoux to the south and Albi to the north surrendered without resistance, thus giving him the last of the important Trencavel towns. The great fear caused by the Crusade was still effective; lesser towns also opened their gates to Simon's little army. Another stroke of good fortune was the death in prison of viscount Raymond Roger. The death seems to have been due to natural causes, but the harshness of the imprisonment was not at all natural for a man of Raymond Roger's rank and it probably contributed to his fatal illness. Simon was now able to strengthen his claims to the viscounty by buying up the rights of Raymond Roger's widow and infant son.

But as time passed, so did the great fear. Lords and towns that had accepted Simon's rule revolted against him; some of

Simon's most trusted companions were killed or taken prisoner. Peter of Aragon refused to accept Simon's homage; the count of Foix, who had allowed Simon to occupy some of his holdings in the plains, became openly hostile and took back one of his occupied castles. It looked as if Simon were going to be nibbled to death. With his small army, he could not garrison every fortress, and yet rebellion was everywhere in the air. A letter of Simon to the pope shows his difficulties: "The lords who took part in the Crusade have left me almost alone surrounded by the enemies of Jesus Christ who occupy the mountains and the hills. I cannot govern this land any longer without your help and that of the faithful. The country has been impoverished by the ravages of war. The heretics have destroyed or abandoned some of their castles, but they have kept others which are stronger and which they intend to defend. I must pay the troops that remain with me at a much higher rate than I would in other wars. I have been able to keep a few soldiers only by doubling their wages."

Simon was saved by his own qualities of courage, tenacity, and ability to make quick decisions, and by the devotion of his companions. Most of his followers came from his own province, the border lands that lay between Normandy and the Ile de France. These men had known each other and worked with each other for many years; the hostility of the Occitanians only drove them closer together. Finally, the rebellion was not coordinated; as before, the southerners could not understand the need for united action. Raymond of Toulouse was still trying to convince the pope and the legates that he was a zealous Catholic; Raymond Roger of Foix was thinking mainly of his own lands; and the lesser lords were each fighting for control of their own little districts. So Simon was able to hold onto the chief fortresses of his viscounty and await the coming of spring.

In the spring Alice de Montfort came south bringing reinforcements to her husband. She probably had only a few hundred men with her, but this was enough to turn the tide. Simon took the offensive and by the end of the year not only had regained all that he had lost, but also had broken the backbone of the rebellion in the Trencavel lands. He was aided as well by successive waves of crusaders who came south to accomplish their forty days of fighting, but he still had to rely on his own small personal following to nail down the victory.

As in 1209, the first stage of the campaign was marked by a deliberate act of terror. Simon took the castle of Bram, in which there were many men who had broken their oaths to him, and, even worse, one of his clerks who had betrayed the castle of Montréal to the rebels. Simon hanged the clerk, and put out the eyes and cut off the nose and upper lip of all the garrison, except for one man, who was left with a single eye to guide his companions to the still unconquered fortress of Cabaret. It is true that Simon had special provocation; two of his own men had been treated in the same way. It is also true that Simon was only following the example of greater men; both Richard Lionheart and Philip Augustus had mutilated hundreds of prisoners. Nevertheless, Simon was much more gentle in his treatment of the garrisons of other castles that surrendered during the next few months, even though these castles also contained traitors. It looks as if he intended to give a warning; in any case, his action was taken as a warning. Several garrisons that might have held out much longer surrendered after a short siege in order to save life and limb.

Most of the other castles and towns that had fallen away during the winter were reoccupied by Simon without much difficulty during the spring and summer of 1210. He strengthened his position still further by taking two of the strongholds that had not yielded during the first campaign, Minerve and Termes. Minerve withstood a siege of seven weeks, then asked for terms. Simon was inclined to be lenient, but the legate Arnaud Amaury insisted that the leaders of the heretics be punished. It was finally agreed that the garrison, the Catholics, and the simple heretics could go free, but that the "perfect" must choose between abjuring their faith or death by fire. Some of Simon's men were annoyed that the Cathars might escape punishment, but the legate knew his opponents; he assured the grumblers that almost none of the "perfect" would recant. He proved to be right; only three women saved themselves. Over one hundred and forty were burned to death; many of them jumped into the blaze of their own accord.

After the fall of Minerve (22 July) came the siege of Termes. This proved to be one of the most difficult operations of the Crusade. At one point a capitulation was negotiated, but just then a large part of Simon's army (forty-day volunteers from the North) decided to go home. The defenders naturally broke the agreement and held out until 22 November, when they tried to escape by night. Some succeeded; some were killed; the commander of the garrison was captured and died in prison.

These two victories practically ended resistance in the southern part of Simon's conquests. There had been much less trouble in the northern part, and a simple military promenade brought promises of obedience from all the important towns, up to and including Albi. In fact, one of the most curious features of the Albigensian Crusades is that very little of the fighting took place in or near Albi. This was due partly to the political skill of the bishop of Albi, who was able to keep on good terms both with his countrymen and with Simon. As lord of most of the town (the viscount had held only a small fortified area), the bishop could protect his people against the Crusades. But there also seems to have been a migration of the more determined heretics to the south. There was no powerful lord in the region of Albi to protect them; there were many in the area that stretched from Toulouse to the Pyrenees. All of Simon's great victories were won in this area, while it was the Inquisition and not the Crusades that ended heresy in Albigeois.

V

THE ENTRAPMENT OF RAYMOND VI

Simon was much more firmly established by early 1211 than he had been at the beginning of 1210. The legitimacy of his authority was becoming recognized; southern lords who did fealty to him gave loyal service, at least for the next few years. His closest companions were also gaining control of the fiefs he had given them and were founding families that have lasted in the region down to the present day. If Simon had been a less ambitious and a less pious man, he might have settled down to a quiet existence as viscount of Béziers and Carcassonne.

There were, however, two problems that worried both Simon and the Church. In the first place, while the Crusade had won some striking victories, it had not greatly reduced the number of heretics. In the second place, Raymond VI of Toulouse still controlled a large part of Occitania and neither Simon nor the Church trusted Raymond. Simon had every reason to fear that Raymond would try to conquer lands that had once been held of him; if a Trencavel viscount of Béziers had always felt threatened by the count of Toulouse, how much more should a French viscount be afraid. The Church, or at least the legates who made Church policy in Occitania, believed that heresy could never be rooted out until Raymond was ousted. Thus the two problems came together: What should be done about Raymond?

With the advantages of hindsight and a firm belief in the devil theory of history, it would be easy to prove that Arnaud Amaury concocted a disgusting plot with the support of Simon, persuaded the reluctant pope to give his consent, and then put Raymond under such pressures that he was forced to choose between submitting to an implacable adversary and fighting a hopeless war. A more reasonable interpretation would be that fallible men, each seeking his own particular goal, more or less by accident caught Raymond in a trap from which he could not escape. Thus it was perfectly natural for Simon to try to protect himself by taking the offensive against Raymond and his followers instead of waiting for an attack. It was perfectly natural for the legates, waiting in vain for any signs of arrests or expulsion of heretics, to conclude that Raymond had no intention of fulfilling his promises, and to excommunicate him once more. It was perfectly natural for Innocent III, in spite of some hesitations, to support his agents and to refuse Raymond's pleas for forgiveness.

All these things are understandable, but they would be easier to understand if Simon, the legates, and the pope had frankly denounced Raymond as an enemy. Instead, they negotiated with him, and gave him hopes of saving himself and his county at the very time they were undermining his position. Raymond was never fairly and openly condemned for any serious fault. He was suspected of complicity in the murder of Pierre de Castelnau, but the complicity was never proved. He was suspected of heresy; this again was never proved, and such evidence as we have makes the charge seem most unlikely. He was accused, quite justly, of not persecuting heretics, but his great rival, Simon, did not have a much better record. Simon would burn the "perfect" when he caught them, but he left the mass of simple Cathar believers alone. No more than Raymond did he wish to rule over a half-populated country. It cannot be repeated too often that the Albigensian Crusades did not wipe out heresy. They killed some of the "perfect"; they ruined many of the protectors of the Cathars, and so they prepared the way for the really effective attack on heresy— the Inquisition. But to blame Raymond who was a compatriot and a friend of many heretics for not doing what the foreigner Simon found impossible smacks of hypocrisy. There was a deep prejudice against Raymond which is hard to explain. He was not a great warrior (no loss in an age of violence); he was not very honest (neither was his sovereign, Philip Augustus); he was overconfident about his skill in negotiation and lacked a sense of political realities. He did not obey the commands of the Church literally; few men of his class did. But with all his weaknesses, at the end of his life he showed remarkable qualities of leadership and gained the devoted support of most men in his country, Catholic and heretic alike. He was not a fool, nor was he an evil man by the standards of his age. His misfortune was that he became a symbol—a symbol for the protection of heresy and the disaffection of Occitania for the Church.

The squeeze on Raymond began within a few months of his penance at St. Gilles. The count was asked again and again to fulfill his promises to suppress the heretics; when he failed to do so the old charges of heresy and complicity in the murder of Pierre de Castelnau were revived. Raymond probably would have had no trouble in clearing himself of these accusations, so the legates were careful never to let the basic issues come to judgment. As one well-informed observer (a nephew of the bishop of Carcassonne) wrote: "Master Thedisius (one of the legates) . . . desired eagerly to find a legal way of keeping the count from proving his innocence. For he saw clearly that if the count were allowed to clear himself . . . all the efforts of the Church in the region would be ruined." The legal trick was to argue that a perjurer could not be allowed to take an oath establishing his innocence. Since Raymond had not kept his promises, he was a perjurer, and so the more serious charges could be kept hanging over his head to the day of his death.

Raymond did his best to break through this legal spider web by invoking the aid of the few men who could have overruled or mollified the legates. He went to Paris, to remind Philip Augustus that the Church was interfering with fiefs held of the crown and that he was a loyal supporter of the king. Philip received him honorably but gave him no encouragement; Philip simply did not want to be involved in the affairs of the South. Raymond then went to Rome, early in 1210, where he again was received with respect and where he had an interview with the pope. He must have made some impression on Innocent, for in several letters the pope suggested that legate Arnaud Amaury and his companions were being a little too harsh, that perhaps it was not Raymond's fault that he had not cleared himself of the charge of heresy. Nevertheless, while Innocent was certainly not as convinced of Raymond's worthlessness as were the legates, he was quite ready to keep up the pressure on the count. If Raymond were really an enemy of the Church, it was a good idea to keep him on the defensive; if he were a contrite but weak-willed sinner then threats of punishment might force him to do his duty. Innocent was willing to listen to Raymond and his supporters, he was willing to ask for further explanations from Arnaud Amaury and Thedisius, but he would not reverse the policy of his legates.

Raymond then played his last card; he sought direct conferences with Simon. He had the support of his brother-in-law, Peter II of Aragon, who had finally accepted Simon's homage for Carcassonne, and who seems to have hoped for a general settlement in Occitania that would have prevented a renewal of the Crusade. Simon and his handful of Frenchmen could be accepted (and eventually absorbed), but any further conquests would upset the delicate balance by which the king of Aragon had at least as much influence in Occitania as the king of France. Peter tried to show his goodwill to both sides by arranging, early in 1211, a marriage of his sister with Raymond's son and a marriage of his son with Simon's daughter. He also reconciled, temporarily, the count of Foix with the French invaders.

All these efforts for pacification, however, were useless. Simon could reach no agreement with Raymond and the legates would not permit any compromise. They wanted to put Raymond in a position in which he would be completely at their mercy. As before, they insisted that he drive the heretics out of his lands, and, as before, Raymond refused. Then an ultimatum was presented to the count. The exact terms of the ultimatum are not clear; they are reported only by one not entirely trustworthy writer. But the general tenor of the demands makes sense: Raymond was to disarm his county, give Simon free entrance to drive heretics out of his lands, and (probably) to go on a Crusade overseas. In other words, since Raymond would not do the job, Simon was to be given power to do it. Raymond might retain his title and some of his revenues, but Simon would be the real ruler of the county.

Whatever the terms, they were completely unacceptable to Raymond; he left the meeting in anger. Peter of Aragon is also said to have been offended, and his subsequent conduct supports the story. On the other hand, whatever the terms they offered, the legates had achieved their objective. Raymond was excommunicated again on 6 February, 1211; Innocent confirmed the sentence on 17 April and ordered the legates to seize Raymond's lands. Simon was to have new opportunities for conquest; the second stage of the Crusade had begun.

Simon began by attacking the last two strongholds in the Trencavel lands, Cabaret and Lavaur. Cabaret fell without a struggle, but Lavaur held out until May 1211. Lavaur was close to Toulouse, and there were divided councils in the city about what should be done. The new bishop was Fulk of Marseilles, appointed in 1206 to take the place of an incompetent predecessor. Fulk was a former troubador who was as zealous for religion as he had formerly been for worldly pleasure. With his encouragement, several hundred men of Toulouse joined the besieging army. Count Raymond certainly did not approve this move, and some of his men, with or without his express orders, took part in the defense. But, as usual, he himself took no decisive stand. He did not really try to block the exit of the soldiers sent by bishop Fulk, and he did not give Lavaur enough aid to enable it to withstand the siege. All he succeeded in doing was to compromise himself still further in the eyes of the Church without having saved an important outpost.

The fall of Lavaur was marked by acts of terror, as was usual at the beginning of Simon's campaigns. This time he had some justification; the commander of the garrison was Aimery of Montréal, who had twice sworn allegiance to Simon and had twice betrayed him. Aimery was hanged, which was perhaps more than he deserved, but eighty other knights were executed, which was certainly going beyond the usual rules of reprisal. The crowning atrocity was the murder of Geralda, the lady of the castle. She was thrown in a well and stones were heaped upon her until she died. Even a Catholic chronicler was horrified by this act; Geralda had been a Cathar but not one of the "perfect," and she was renowned for her acts of charity. At the same time, some four hundred of the "perfect" were burned, one of the largest mass executions of the Crusades. It seems to have taught the Cathar leaders a lesson; after the fall of Lavaur, with only a few exceptions, they ceased taking refuge in fortified towns. This change in tactics is one of the reasons why Simon's final victory did not greatly weaken the Cathar Church.

The massacre of Lavaur had the expected effect; dozens of towns and castles in the region of Toulouse surrendered. Simon seemed to be planning an encirclement of the city, which was a sensible plan, but for once in his life he lost patience and took an unnecessary risk. The usual crowd of summer crusaders had joined him, the legate Arnaud Amaury and bishop Fulk were pressing him to act, and so he tried a direct attack on Toulouse. But Toulouse was not Béziers or Carcassonne; it was one of the largest towns of Occitania, with a population of over 25,000 people. Even with his summer reinforcements, Simon could not hope to surround it, and there could be no shortage of water in a city bordered by the Garonne. The only chance for the besiegers was that the Catholic citizens would open the gates, and once more it was proved that the Occitanians paid little attention to religious differences. Toulouse had struggled for a century to obtain virtual independence; it was not going to accept the rule of a Montfort count or an authoritarian bishop just because some of its inhabitants were Cathars. When told that they would be spared if they renounced their allegiance to Raymond VI, the men of Toulouse answered that they would not betray their count. This was honorable; it was also good sense. Raymond had favored the citizens and his whole position in western Occitania was based on the support of Toulouse; the city could be sure that its liberties were safe as long as he was count. As events were to prove, the autonomy of the city and the fortunes of Raymond were inextricably intertwined, and the substitution of a foreign line of counts started a steady erosion of Toulousan freedom.

Simon soon saw that he had little chance of success and broke off the siege. He probably would have done so in any case, but his decision was speeded by the fact that Raymond had at last begun to fight. For the moment, with the capital of his western lands under attack, there was no reason for Raymond to carry on his policy of negotiation. And for the moment, almost all the lords of western Occitania realized their common danger and were ready to help Raymond. If Simon had waited much longer, he would have been caught between the walls of the city and a strong relief force.

As it was he slipped away, and tried to keep the enemy off balance by quick thrusts to the south and to the north. He ravaged the lands of the count of Foix right up to the gates of his castle, thus momentarily confusing one of the best fighters among his opponents. He moved north to Cahors, where he reeived the homage of the bishop and his men. This expedition may have hurt Raymond's pride, but it added little to Simon's strength. Cahors was one of those dioceses of northern Occitania where the bishop was the most powerful lord; in fact, the bishop of Cahors claimed to be count of Quercy. He was more interested in gaining independence than in helping the conquest of Toulouse; as soon as Simon left, the bishop did homage to the king of France.

Meanwhile, the southern barons were gathering their forces. The counts of Foix and Comminges, the viscount of Béarn, Savary de Mauléon, seneschal of Aquitaine for the king of England, and many lesser men joined Raymond. The army was not composed solely of Raymond's vassals, and many of Raymond's vassals were also vassals of the king of Aragon or the king of England. We know that Peter of Aragon was hostile to Simon, and John had no reason to love a supporter of Innocent III; both kings may have encouraged their men to join the southern army. Besides the barons and knights there were a number of mercenaries, but they were all southerners, and proved fairly reliable, while the mercenaries that Simon had hired often deserted or went off on plundering expeditions.

No real estimate of numbers can be given, but fall was setting in, most of the temporary crusaders had gone home, and Simon must have had a much smaller force than his opponents. Nevertheless, in 1211–1212, as in the previous winter,

Simon showed what could be done with disciplined troops under a determined commander. The campaign that followed the coalition of the southern barons was perhaps the most brilliant of Simon's career. He was always on the defensive, he lost castle after castle, and yet he was never beaten and he never lost an essential position. Conversely, the campaign of late 1211 and early 1212 revealed again the fatal weakness of the Occitanians. If they had at last agreed on the need for joint action, they were no more capable than before of establishing a unified command. Even when they were together in the field they did not coordinate their actions, and so their superior numbers were useless.

The tone of the whole campaign was set by the first engagement at Castelnaudary (September 1211). Simon had concentrated the bulk of his forces in Castelnaudary, on the border between his lands and those of Raymond. The fortifications were weak and the southern army began a siege. But when Raymond Roger of Foix tried to intercept a column coming to reinforce Simon, he received no support from Raymond of Toulouse. The count of Foix very nearly won the battle by himself, but a charge by Simon rescued most of the crusaders. It seems likely that if Raymond of Toulouse had thrown all his strength into the fight Simon might have been badly defeated; as it was, Raymond lost one of his best chances to save his position. The besiegers were not driven off, but they were discouraged, and eventually gave up their attempt to take Castelnaudary. The rest of the winter season was taken up with meaningless actions; small victories by the counts of Foix and Toulouse did not hurt Simon; small victories by Simon did not stop southern resistance.

With the coming of the spring of 1212, the usual flow of crusaders from the North began and Simon could once more take the offensive. He resumed his plan of encircling Toulouse. He first occupied the region around Agen, a fief held by Raymond of the king of England. He then took Moissac, where he had to share the rule of the town with the abbot. With Agen, Cahors, Moissac, and Albi in his hands, Simon held most of the key points to the northeast, the north, and the northwest of Toulouse. His earlier conquests had given him control of the southern and southeastern approaches. He now moved to close the last gap on the southwest by attacking the lands of the count of Comminges. With the capture of Auterive and Muret the circle was practically complete.

In this campaign Simon had shown his usual qualities of quick decision, fast movement, and just enough brutality to persuade besieged towns to surrender in order to avoid sacking and killing. He had also shown a good deal of audacity. Granting that John of England was fully occupied with his quarrels with the pope and with Philip Augustus, he still had many loyal supporters in the region around Bordeaux; it was a little risky to invade Agenais. As subsequent events were to show, the English kings stubbornly maintained their claim to this province. Granting that the count of Comminges had aided Raymond, it was still risky to irritate him by seizing his outlying lands. This might have involved Simon in a war in the Pyrenees, a region in which he had no real interest. But both gambles succeeded. John's followers did not react and the count of Comminges made little resistance. At the end of 1212 Simon was in the most favorable military position he had yet enjoyed.

Raymond of Toulouse, on the other hand, had lost ground, both physically and morally. The strategic encirclement of Toulouse was not a blockade, but it did hamper communications with Aquitaine and with the counts of the Pyrenees. Raymond's income had been somewhat reduced and some of his vassals were no longer ready to fight for him. Worst of all, Raymond had been forced into the position of making war on the crusaders and on their leader, Simon de Montfort. It was difficult for him to argue that he was not protecting heretics when he was fighting the men who sought to exterminate heretics. Raymond desperately needed to be reconciled to the Church; the events of 1211 and 1212 were not calculated to make the papal legates feel inclined to grant him absolution.

THE TRIUMPH OF SIMON DE MONTFORT

Simon had been almost too successful during the campaigns of 1212. On the one hand, Innocent III was beginning to wonder if the Crusade should be prolonged. The protectors of the heretics had been chastised; the strongest of them, Raymond of Toulouse, was apparently ready to make serious concessions to the Church. Innocent had other problems: a hostile emperor in Germany, an English king who had seized most of the property of the Church in his realm, a Moslem sultan in possession of the Holy City of Jerusalem, and a crucial campaign against the Moors of Spain. Was it really sensible to use crusaders to enable Simon de Montfort to enlarge his principality when they were so badly needed elsewhere?

On the other hand, the fear of French domination was growing in Occitania. Simon as viscount of Béziers could be tolerated; the prospect of Simon as count of Toulouse with fiefs extending from the borders of Aquitaine into the mountains of Provence was something else. Simon had already indicated that he expected far more service and much greater obedience from his vassals than was customary in the South; he made this attitude explicit in the Statutes of Pamiers, drawn up by an assembly that met in November–December, 1212. The statutes gave extensive privileges to the clergy and sought to guarantee the safety of the lives and property of commoners. But their main purpose was to introduce French feudal law into the South. There was to be no more dividing of fiefs more or less equally among the heirs; the eldest son was to have the lion's share. All French vassals were to give extensive amounts of military service, and were to grant rear-fiefs only to French knights. Southerners who were loyal to Simon were to give only the services formerly owed, but it was implied that these services would be carefully examined and demanded in full. The custom of Paris was to determine all matters connected with feudal tenures.

For men of the South these statutes were both a threat and a provocation. They were a threat because if they were fully enforced they would make Simon immensely strong, stronger than any possible rival in Occitania. They were a provocation because they would wipe out local customs and impose an alien set of laws. For men of the Middle Ages one's law was part of one's birthright, one's property, one's sense of identity. To deprive a district of its own customs was tyranny, robbery, cultural genocide. Simon had realized that there would be protests against his new laws. He had tried to avoid the danger by summoning members of the clergy, the nobility, and a few townsmen to the meeting at Pamiers, and by having the statutes drafted by a committee of four clerics, four northern knights, and four southerners. This was very advanced constitutional procedure (England was not to reach this level for several generations), but not very effective propaganda. The statutes were French statutes, Simon's statutes, and everyone knew it. In the end they remained in force only for the handful of French families that established themselves in the Béziers-Carcassonne region.

Even utterly orthodox and pious Catholics felt that Simon had gone too far and had become too strong. Chief of these was Peter II of Aragon, a ruler who had already shown some displeasure with Simon and who was convinced by the end of 1212 that French expansion must be stopped. Peter had many reasons to be concerned about the balance of power in Occitania. The mountain counts and Simon himself were vassals of the king of Aragon for some of their holdings; both Raymond of Toulouse and his son had married princesses of the Aragonese royal family. Peter had acquired Montpellier, one of the greatest southern cities, by marriage; his brother and nephew were counts of Provence.[1] Peter's own county of Catalonia belonged to the Occitanian cultural sphere, as we have

---

[1] Provence, like the rest of Occitania, was so fragmented that it is almost impossible to describe the political situation there. The *marquisate* of Provence (mostly to the north) was held by Raymond of Toulouse; the *county* of Provence (mostly to the south and including Marseilles) was held by the House of Aragon.

seen, and its dependency of Roussillon was on the northern side of the Pyrenees. But while Peter had a very substantial position in Occitania, it was not a strong position; his lands were scattered and his vassals were not reliable. Like everyone else in the country, Peter had reason to fear the emergence of a powerful Montfort state. And besides these political reasons, Peter seems to have had real sympathy with the house of Toulouse and some feeling of identity with Occitanian culture and language.

The doubts of Innocent III and the anxieties of Peter II grew steadily during the year 1212. In April or in May, Innocent wrote to his legates, asking them once more to give Raymond a chance to clear himself and forbidding them to confiscate Raymond's lands. These orders very likely had some connection with the great Crusade that was being launched against the Moors of Spain. Innocent clearly thought this expedition more important than the war against Raymond, and even his implacable legate, Arnaud Amaury, seems to have been of the same opinion. Arnaud Amaury, now archbishop of Narbonne, led a contingent of troops to Spain; many others, who might have joined Simon, followed Arnaud Amaury's example.

The Spanish Crusade was a brilliant success. On 16 July, 1212, the Spanish Moslems were crushed in the battle of Las Navas de Tolosa. The victory was won by a combined force of French crusaders and troops from Navarre, Castile, and Aragon, but the hero of the combat was Peter II. He was hailed throughout Europe as the conqueror of the Moors and the champion of Christendom. His prestige reached a point where even Innocent III had to pay serious attention to his requests, and Innocent, for reasons of his own, was inclined to listen to Peter's suggestions. The pope realized that the victory of Las Navas de Tolosa had shattered the power of the Spanish Moslems and had given the Christians a greater opportunity than they had ever had during the long centuries of the Reconquest. The essential thing was to keep the Moors off balance, to prevent them from regrouping and bringing in reinforcements from Africa. Steady pressure could (and in the event did) bring almost all of Spain under Christian rule. The conquest of southern Spain was worth more than the humiliation of a handful of Occitanian counts. Was it worth running the slightest risk of weakening the push in Spain in order to gain unnecessary victories over Raymond of Toulouse? The heretics had had their lesson; the Church in Occitania was stronger than it had been for generations. Innocent had dismissed the weak and lukewarm bishops who had done nothing about heresy; key positions were now held by his own men, such as Fulk at Toulouse, Thedisius at Agde, and Arnaud Amaury at Narbonne. The pope could trust these prelates to keep up steady pressure on the Cathars. Why not declare the Crusade at an end?

These are the arguments that Peter must have used and that Innocent, for a time, accepted. On 15 January, 1213, the pope wrote a remarkable letter to Arnaud Amaury. "Foxes *were* destroying the vineyard of the Lord in Provence [Occitania]; they *have been captured*.[2] Now we must guard aganist a greater danger. We hear that the Saracens of Spain are preparing a new army to avenge their defeat. . . . Moreover, the Holy Land needs assistance." Therefore, the legate was to stop preaching the Crusade and work with Peter to bring peace to the land.

On the same day Simon was sent an even more irritating letter. "The illustrious king of Aragon complains that, not content with opposing heretics, you have led crusaders against Catholics, that you have shed the blood of innocent men and have wrongfully invaded the lands of his vassals, the counts of Foix and Comminges, Gaston of Béarn, while the king was making war on the Saracens and though the people of these lands were never suspected of heresy. . . ." Therefore, Simon was to restore all that he had unjustly seized, and the indulgences granted for his Crusade were henceforth valid only if the recipients went to fight in Spain or in the Holy Land.

Peter followed up this diplomatic success by forming a series of alliances with the lords who were threatened by Simon —the counts of Toulouse, Foix, and Comminges and the viscount of Béarn. This was not an unmixed blessing for the counts—Peter began to assert his tenuous rights as overlord even in remote Provence—but the danger from Peter was far

---

[2] I have italicized the verbs to show that the pope was thinking of the Crusade as a completed operation.

less than the danger from Simon. Peter was willing to risk his reputation and his life to save Occitania from conquest by the French. If he succeeded, he would be the greatest lord in the country, but he would be a ruler who sympathized with the southern way of life. Moreover, his power would be strictly limited. The lands of the crown of Aragon were only loosely united, and the victory at Las Navas de Tolosa had opened the road to the conquest of the Moorish kingdom of Valencia. Peter and his heirs were going to be very busy in Spain; they could not expand their holdings in the peninsula and at the same time dominate Occitania.

Peter's maneuvers worried Simon and horrified the papal representatives in the South. A council held at Lavaur in January 1213 held fast to the old policies: Raymond was not to be trusted; heresy could never be extirpated until he was driven out of the country; Simon de Montfort was the only man who could save the Church in the South. The council sent envoys to Innocent III; most of its members wrote individual letters as well. They must have been very persuasive, for in May Innocent reversed himself completely. Peter was scolded for having misinformed and misled the pope, and the Crusade against the heretics and their supporters was declared legitimate and desirable. Raymond's enemies had won again.

Nevertheless, Innocent's vacillations had seriously endangered Simon de Montfort. The temporary downgrading of the Crusade reduced the number of recruits coming down from the North; Simon's army was very small during the summer of 1213 when it should have been at its peak. On the other hand, the pope's belated rebuke of Peter and other allies of Raymond had little effect. Gascons, men from the mountain counties, and dispossessed vassals of the Trencavels joined with Raymond of Toulouse and with Peter's Aragonese forces. All of western Occitania was on the march against Simon.

Simon showed his usual skill and prudence. He concentrated his forces and abandoned most of his outposts. He kept a small garrison in Muret, a position that controlled communications between Toulouse and the Pyrenees. When Muret was attacked he moved to its defense with all his available troops and entered the town on 11 September.

His position seemed hopeless, even to the churchmen who were the most ardent supporters of the Crusade. All estimates of numbers are suspect, but Peter had at least twice as many men as Simon—say 8,000 against 4,000.[8] Most of the sources agree that Peter allowed Simon to enter Muret without opposition in the hope of trapping him there instead of having to pursue him from place to place. This was a sensible strategy; all the allies had to do was to stay in their fortified camp and let Simon choose between a retreat that might turn into a rout or a hopeless attack on superior forces.

---

[8] Ferdinand Lot, *L'art militaire et les armées au moyen age*, I, 214–216, gives the most thorough discussion of the size of the two armies. Austin P. Evans, "The Albigensian Crusade," in *A History of the Crusades* (ed. K. M. Setton), II, 302, estimates that Simon had 800–1000 mounted men and his opponents 2000–4000.

The plan was good, but Peter found it hard to follow. Raymond of Toulouse, not a very belligerent character, urged the king to await Simon's assault in a good defensive position, but he was hooted down. When Simon, on 12 September, led his forces out of Muret, the count of Foix, followed by Peter of Aragon, moved out to meet the enemy.

Once more Simon showed his great qualities as a general and once more the Occitanians revealed their fatal weakness, their inability to concert their actions. Simon, with his well-disciplined troops, and his remarkable sense of timing, was able to strike each division of the enemy separately. Though he was outnumbered overall, in the actual fighting his troops were probably as numerous as those of the units they were engaging at the moment. First, the knights of the count of Foix were swept aside; then, the crusaders joined battle with the army of the king of Aragon. This was a hard fight; the young Raymond (son of the count) said that it sounded like the felling of a forest of trees by a corps of axemen. Some of Peter's auxiliaries fled in terror, and the king himself was killed in a hand-to-hand struggle with French knights. This ended the battle. The reluctant warrior, Raymond VI, did not strike a blow, and the Toulousan infantry was cut down in the field, or driven into the Garonne and drowned.

The slaughter of the men of Toulouse made a strong impression throughout France. The northern poet, Guillaume le Breton, in his life of Philip Augustus, gave several pages to the battle of Muret and reached a peak of savage exultation when he described the last stage of the combat: "The men of Toulouse tried to defend themselves within their camp, but soon had to give ground. Unable to resist the furious charge they retreated shamefully before their enemies. Like a wolf who, having broken into a sheepfold by night, does not care to slake his thirst or fill his belly with meat, but is content to tear open the throats of the sheep, adding dead to the dead, lapping up blood with his tongue, so the army consecrated to God thrust through their enemies and with avenging swords executed the wrath of God on the people who offended Him doubly by deserting the faith and by associating with heretics. No one wasted time in taking booty, or prisoners, but they reddened their swords with heavy blows. . . . On that day the power and virtue of the French shone forth clearly; they sent seventeen thousand men to the swamps of hell." Guillaume could exult, but Toulouse did not forget or forgive the massacre.

Muret was not a great battle, nor, as it turned out, even a decisive battle. Raymond VI and his son escaped, to renew the struggle with more success five years later. But at the moment Simon de Montfort was triumphant. He had defeated the combined forces of Occitania; he had eliminated forever the threat of Aragonese intervention; he had made it impossible for the Raymonds to defend Toulouse. He had asked for the judgment of God and God had judged in his favor.

Nevertheless, it took almost two years for Simon to reap

all the fruits of his victory. Innocent III was still uncertain about his policy; he had a lingering respect for the rights of Raymond and some doubts as to whether the aggrandizement of Simon was the best way to eliminate heresy in Occitania. Until the pope made up his mind, Simon could not take over Toulouse. In addition, Narbonne, one of the most important cities of the region, was not eager to accept Simon's rule. Narbonne had long been a problem for the counts of Toulouse and it was just as troublesome to Simon. Though the count of Toulouse was titular duke of Narbonne, actual power in the city was divided among the archbishop, the viscount, and the consuls chosen by the burghers. The viscount resisted Simon by force of arms and the archbishop was now the old papal legate, Arnaud Amaury. Arnaud Amaury proved as zealous in defending his rights as an ecclesiastical prince as he had in prosecuting Raymond, and Simon was not permitted to take over Narbonne. Finally, Montpellier remained a possession of the House of Aragon, and refused to admit Simon within its walls. Thus Simon, excluded from the three largest cities of Occitania, could only roam around the edges of the fiefs of the count of Toulouse. He raided the lands of the count of Foix once more; he received the submission of the count of Rodez; he strengthened his position in Agenais and Quercy by subduing rebellious barons and recalcitrant towns. He pushed to the Rhône and even tried to take over Raymond's rights as marquis of Provence. This last move was probably a mistake. Provence, as we saw earlier, was a part of the Empire, not of the kingdom of France, and the Crusade had never been directed against the lords of Provence. The grudging acceptance of Simon's overlordship in Provence gave him no real power and left bitter memories behind. The rebellion which was to destroy Simon and the Montfort claims to the South began in Provence.

Raymond VI had not given up all hope of winning some military successes. Early in 1214 his mercenaries succeeded in capturing his younger brother, Baldwin. Baldwin had grown up in the court of the king of France[4] but had served Raymond faithfully until the Crusade began. In 1211, however, he had gone over to Simon de Montfort, perhaps thinking that a completely orthodox, northern-bred member of the House of Toulouse would have a good claim to the county if anything happened to Raymond. He served Simon well, notably at the battle of Muret, and Raymond hated him as only brothers can hate. The count of Foix wanted satisfaction for his defeat at Muret, and the surviving knights of the household of Peter of Aragon sought vengeance for their master. Baldwin was condemned to death as a traitor and was hanged immediately. No one seems to have considered this act an atrocity. The French praised Baldwin's courage in meeting death, but they never blamed Raymond for the execution as they had for the assassination

---

[4] Baldwin's mother was Constance, sister of Louis VII of France. Baldwin was born while his mother was visiting the French court and was left there to be educated because Constance was on very bad terms with her husband, Raymond V of Toulouse.

of Pierre de Castelnau. The Occitanians rejoiced publicly over Baldwin's punishment. To betray one's brother and lord was still one of the worst possible crimes. Baldwin was unlucky, but few men would have said that he was guiltless.

Raymond also made a fruitless attack on Moissac, but for the most part, he stayed on the defensive, while Simon consolidated his gains. During 1214 it became more and more apparent that Raymond did not have the strength to resist a direct attack by the Frenchman. Only diplomatic intervention by Philip Augustus or Innocent III could save him.

Simon also had to wait for the decisions of his two superiors, the pope and the king of France. Both Innocent III and Philip Augustus hesitated to give full authority over the vast holdings of the House of Toulouse to this ambitious and dangerously able baron of the Ile de France. Innocent had some reason to wonder whether Simon cared as much about destroying heresy as he did about acquiring land. Philip Augustus wanted to be sure that his rights as suzerain were respected, and he must have wondered whether a strong count of Toulouse would really be preferable to the weak Raymond VI.

Innocent and Philip were both too busy during 1214 to make up their minds about Raymond and Simon. Innocent was preparing the great Lateran Council of 1215; Philip was preparing his final, victorious campaign against John of England. Meanwhile a new papal legate, Peter of Benevento, was left to make interim decisions. He seems to have held the balance fairly even; he absolved all those who sought reconciliation with the Church, he confirmed all of Simon's earlier conquests, but he refused to give Simon either the title of count of Toulouse or the city itself. By this policy the legate found himself, for the moment, in a stronger position than Simon. During the spring of 1214 the counts of Foix and Comminges, the burgesses of Toulouse, and Raymond VI himself threw themselves on the mercy of the Church and promised to obey all orders of the pope. Raymond VI transferred all his rights to his son and offered to cede his lands to the Church. Peter of Benevento seems to have hoped to use these submissions to build up an ecclesiastical state or states in the South to balance the power of Simon de Montfort. Thus at Toulouse bishop Fulk was given possession of the count's castle, and the key to the city, and the abbot of St. Thibéry was given custody of the castle of Foix. Even if these were only temporary measures, they might have forced Simon to recognize the suzerainty of the Church before he took over the remainder of the lands of the count of Toulouse. And there was always a possibility that young Raymond might receive some of his father's holdings as a fief of the Church.

But the new group of southern bishops, who, unlike their predecessors, were fervent opponents of heresy, vehemently opposed the suggested limitations on Simon's power. They realized that in the long struggle against the Cathars and their friends, Simon was the one man who had gained an unbroken series of victories, the one man who had the toughness and the determination to create a political climate in which the Church could wipe out its enemies. They all feared a division of power in the South; many of them must have realized that ecclesiastical lordships were apt to be weak and that laymen who held fiefs of the Church were not always obedient vassals. In a council held at Montpellier in January 1215 they advised the legate to give Toulouse and all the other lands conquered by the crusaders to Simon. When Peter of Benevento answered that only the pope could make such a decision, the council sent a delegation to Rome asking that Simon be made sole ruler of the lands of Raymond. Innocent postponed final decision to the General Council which was about to meet, but he went a long way toward meeting the wishes of the bishops by granting Simon *de facto* administrative rights in the county of Toulouse.

Innocent may have made this concession because he had learned that the king of France was at last taking an interest in the affairs of the South. Philip Augustus had just won a double victory; he had defeated Otto IV of Germany and some rebellious French barons at Bouvines, while his son had pushed back the army which John of England was leading up from the south. Philip no longer had any enemy to fear; he could devote himself to consolidating the conquests that had more than tripled the size of his domain. He was an unscrupulous and not very pious man with a keen sense of political realities. He had no particular interest in combatting heresy and he knew perfectly well that he could not hope to annex parts of Occitania; he already had all that he could handle in the

North. Nevertheless, it was just as well to remind Simon, the legate, and the pope that Toulouse was a fief held of the crown of France and that the king had rights there that should not be ignored. He found the ideal solution; he allowed his son Louis to go to the South to fulfill the crusading vow that he had made years before. Louis was a good general; he also had all the moral qualities that his father lacked. He was pious, upright, and honorable, the sort of man who would be completely acceptable to both Montfort and the Church.

Nevertheless, the legate showed some anxiety and warned Louis, when he arrived in April 1215, not to try to interfere with the decisions that had already been made. Simon was less worried, and with reason. He belonged to the old aristocracy of the Ile de France, the group whom the Capetians trusted above all others. Simon and Louis were fellow-countrymen, in the closest sense of the word; they understood each other and got on well together. In spite of the legate's warnings, Louis did interfere in southern affairs, and always in favor of Simon. As heir of France, he could hardly avoid being asked to arbitrate disputes, and his open support of Simon did much to strengthen the latter's position. Thus, in the continuing dispute between Simon and Arnaud Amaury over Narbonne, Louis ordered the fortifications of the town destroyed and made the viscount and the town officials swear allegiance to Simon.

The most decisive action, however, was taken against Toulouse. Louis ordered the city to destroy its walls, fill up its moats, and prepare to accept the government of Simon de Montfort. Raymond VI and his son took refuge in England and on 15 May Simon, Louis, and the legate entered the town. Simon established his residence in the count's castle, an act that symbolized his final triumph. He was now ruler of all Raymond's lands from Agenais to the Rhône, from Quercy to the Pyrenees. He still needed papal and royal confirmation of his conquests, but this was soon to come.

The Fourth Lateran Council, one of the greatest ecclesiastical meetings of the Middle Ages, held its first sessions in November 1215. The Council had a long agenda, but one of its chief concerns was the problem of heresy and the fate of the count of Toulouse. Innocent had no difficulty in securing approval of the Crusade and of the doctrine that a lord who failed to root out heresy could be replaced by a good Catholic who was willing to do what the Church required. But while it was easy to approve these general principles, it was difficult to apply them to the specific case of Raymond VI and his son. Raymond had strong support among the clergy—not least from his old enemy Arnaud Amaury, who was so irritated by Simon's claim to Narbonne that he sought to thwart him by reinstating his rival in Toulouse. Raymond, moreover, had twice done penance; he had submitted himself completely to the orders of the Church, and it seemed unfair to punish him further. And if Raymond VI had sinned so grievously that he deserved to lose all his lands, his son was guiltless and should not suffer for the misdeeds of his father. These argu-

ments weighed heavily on Innocent, as did his personal rela-
tionships with the count of Toulouse and his family. Innocent
probably had no illusions about Raymond's ability or strength
of character, but he found him a civilized and decent man, and
he pitied the attractive young Raymond.

The pressures around the pope were great. He resolved
them by applying the formula that had been urged on him for
years by his legates. The Raymonds would never extirpate
heresy and there could be no security for the Church if authority were divided between Simon and the Raymonds. Therefore the pope decided on, and the Council approved, the granting
of all conquered lands to Simon de Montfort. Raymond was
to have a pension of four hundred marks a year, and the lands
that he had not lost—chiefly his holdings in Provence—were
to be guarded by the Church until his son was of age to receive them. (As on other occasions, this last decree fell into the
grave error of confusing lands of the Empire with lands of the
kingdom of France. Raymond VI never lost effective control of
his holdings in Provence and the emperor Frederick II never
recognized the right of the Church to intervene there.) As far
as the Church was concerned, Simon was now count of Toulouse, duke of Narbonne, and viscount of Béziers and Carcassonne.

This was very well, but Simon had a healthy respect for
and real loyalty to his king. He hastened to Paris and in April
1216 did homage to Philip Augustus for his fiefs. Philip confirmed him in his claims to all lands conquered from Raymond

VI, recognized all his titles, and ordered all his subjects to aid Simon whenever he needed help. The Albigensian Crusade had reached a successful conclusion. A loyal supporter of the Church held all of middle Occitania; the mountain counts were still threatened with the loss of their lands in spite of their abject submission; no one was left to threaten Simon or to protect the heretics. Few medieval wars had led to such apparently decisive results.

VII

THE OCCITANIAN
COUNTERATTACK

Simon reached the height of his power in 1216. He had been officially recognized as count of Toulouse, viscount of Béziers, and (in spite of Arnaud Amaury) duke of Narbonne. In addition, he had occupied most of the county of Comminges and had arranged marriages for his sons that might have brought more Occitanian lands into the family. It is true that the Raymonds had retained a foothold in the northern part of the old county of Toulouse and that they had fairly extensive holdings on the east of the Rhône in Provence. It was also true that the count of Foix had saved his county by agreeing to accept a papal inquiry into his conduct, and that the dispossessed count of Comminges was by no means reconciled to his fate. But if the three counts had been unable to resist Simon when their possessions and their prestige were intact, what hope did they have after a long string of defeats and a condemnation by an Ecumenical Council? It looked as if Simon could spend the rest of his life consolidating his position and that he could hand on his principality intact to his eldest son, Amaury.

Actually, Simon was less secure than it appeared because he lacked solid military support. Thousands of Frenchmen had taken part in the Crusade, but very few had settled in the South. And, except for the handful of Frenchmen, there was no one with military experience in the county of Toulouse who could be entirely trusted. The most zealous supporters of the heretics had been killed or exiled, but Occitanians who had bowed before the storm formed the vast majority of Simon's vassals. Such men were covertly hostile to Simon; they were not going to revolt of their own accord, but, if someone else started a revolt, they were not going to get themselves killed defending Simon. And the inhabitants of the larger towns, who were essential for defensive operations, were even more hostile to Simon than were the nobles. They resented French domination; they feared for their privileges; and many of them were sincerely loyal to the House of Toulouse and were ready to fight to restore its rights.

Simon had never been popular in the South; he was not one of those conquerors who knows how to gain the cooperation, however grudging, of a defeated people. This weakness had endangered him several times in the past, but the danger had always been averted by outside support. After 1215, however, outside support dwindled. There was, for a while, less interest in Crusades. Why should a French army have to march South every summer to rescue Simon from his difficulties? Innocent III died in July 1216; his successor, Honorius III, was a much milder man who preferred negotiation to war. The new generation of southern bishops was zealous for the faith but equally zealous in protecting the rights of its churches. Many prelates quarreled with Simon; we have already seen the case of Arnaud Amaury of Narbonne. There was much less pressure from the episcopate on the pope than there had been in 1215, much less eagerness to protect Simon at all costs. Finally, the French royal family was particularly uninterested in the problems of the South during the period that followed Simon's investiture as count of Toulouse. John of England was in serious trouble in 1216; his repudiation of Magna Carta had touched off a baronial uprising. The rebellion opened up interesting possibilities for both Philip Augustus and his son. Philip hoped to gain full possession of the disputed county of Poitou; Louis was urged by the disaffected barons to claim the throne of England. In spite of the vehement opposition of the Church, ending in excommunication, Louis invaded England and continued his campaign even after John's death in October 1216. The affair was not resolved until late in 1217 when Louis did penance and promised to give the Church one-tenth of his income for two years. Meanwhile, Louis remained excommunicated and on cool terms with the pope and his legates. Thus, during the crucial years when Simon's power was being overthrown, neither Philip nor Louis was in any position to intervene in Toulouse. Moreover, Louis' expedition to England attracted many fighting men who might otherwise have been available for the war in the South.

Simon's troubles started when Raymond VI and his son, Raymond VII,[1] landed at Marseilles in April 1216. Marseilles was an independent city-state, under no particular obligation to the Raymonds, but it greeted them with extravagant professions of loyalty and support. Equally enthusiastic promises of aid came from the rest of Provence and especially from the northern regions where the Raymonds had their principal holdings. The nobles and burghers of Provence had seen just enough of Simon to fear his rule and not enough of him to fear his power. The Raymonds could protect them against the threat of French domination without interfering with the virtual independence of barons and towns. In less than a month a large army was gathered at Avignon, looking for an opportunity to injure Simon's cause. Raymond VI went off to Aragon to seek help in starting an uprising in Toulouse, leaving Raymond VII in command of the forces in Provence.

The opportunity that the Raymonds had been seeking came in May, when the strategically situated town of Beau-

---

[1] As we have seen, in an attempt to save Toulouse for his family, Raymond VI had surrendered all his rights of government to his son. This was pure fiction at first, but by 1216 young Raymond was taking over real responsibilities in military operations and in government, and his role increased steadily during the remainder of his father's life (down to 1222). He was universally referred to as "the young count," and the narrative will be clearer if we begin calling him Raymond VII in 1216.

caire on the west bank of the Rhône[2] put itself under their lordship. Young Raymond crossed the river at once and occupied the town, but the French garrison, under one of Simon's ablest lieutenants, was able to take refuge in the citadel. Simon's brother and son rushed with what forces they could find to Beaucaire, where Simon joined them early in June.

Now a double siege began: Raymond VII sought to starve out the garrison of the citadel, while Simon tried to cut off Raymond's supplies and so lure him into a pitched battle. But Simon could not blockade the town on the river side, and Raymond and his troops lived in luxury while the French were on very short rations. Nor could Simon tempt Raymond into ill-advised sorties; the Occitanians had finally learned that lesson. In desperation Simon made three assaults on the town; each time his men, though they fought bravely, were thrown back. Finally, on 24 August, Simon gave up. In return for safe exit of the troops in the citadel, Simon lifted the siege and abandoned the town and its fortifications to Raymond VII.

In a purely material sense, the loss of Beaucaire did little damage to Simon. He had held the town less than two years and it was far removed from his real centers of power—Béziers, Carcassonne, and Toulouse. But in terms of morale, the fall of Beaucaire was a disaster. For the first time an Occitanian army

---

[2] Though Beaucaire was west of the Rhône, it could be considered part of Provence. It had been held by the archbishop of Arles, whose cathedral city was certainly in Provence, and had only recently (1215) been given to Simon as a fief by the archbishop.

had shown itself equal to the French in discipline, unity, and determination. For the first time Simon had failed to win one of his miraculous victories; the legend of his invincibility was shattered. A wave of excitement ran through Occitania; the troubadors mocked Simon, and the exiled and the dispossessed began to weave new plots. Not everyone was ready to rebel, but everyone was waiting to see who next would bait the old lion.

Next was the city of Toulouse, a community that had many reasons to love the Raymonds and many reasons—not least the slaughter of its infantry at Muret—to hate Simon. The news that Raymond VI was raising troops in Spain and marching for the Pyrenees stirred the citizens and worried the Montforts. Simon moved rapidly toward the west and Raymond VI retired equally rapidly into Spain. But Toulouse was restless—just how restless is hard to say. Certainly there had been some plotting with the Raymonds and some acts of disobedience, but Simon would have been well advised to ignore petty misdeeds and to punish only a few conspicuously guilty individuals. Instead, he blamed the whole town and then refused to accept the apologies and offers of reparation of the leading citizens. While he was still demanding more abject forms of submission, a riot broke out which soon turned into a rebellion. Simon's soldiers were driven from the streets to take refuge in the cathedral; for a brief period the rebels were masters of the city. But they soon realized that Simon held many citizens as hostages, that their fortifications were destroyed, and that the largest part of Simon's army was still undefeated. The bishop and the abbot of St. Sernin acted as peacemakers, and Simon agreed to pardon the city in return for the enormous sum of 30,000 marks. This was more than enough to support a large army for a year, and Simon's shortage of money and men was certainly one reason for inflicting such a heavy fine. The fine was a mistake, nevertheless; Toulouse became even more hostile to the Montforts and its next revolt was far more serious.

For the rest of 1216 and early 1217 Simon had to deal with a series of small uprisings and acts of defiance. He held his own, but only at the cost of almost ceaseless campaigning; both he and his troops must have become a little weary. And in the summer of 1217, encouraged by the arrival of a few crusaders from the North, Simon crossed the Rhône to punish the lords of Provence who had supported Raymond VII at Beaucaire. Like his other interventions in Provence, this expedition proved to be ill-advised. Once again Simon moved far away from the key area of his principality, and this time his enemies were to take full advantage of his absence.

Toulouse was still smoldering with anger against the Montforts, but the leading citizens realized that only a carefully planned rebellion had any chance of success. They offered to surrender the city to Raymond VI if he would bring sufficient forces to hold it, and for once in his life Raymond acted with decision. He raised what troops he could in Spain and crossed the Pyrenees, where he was joined by the counts of

Foix and Comminges, and other mountain barons. The army marched straight on Toulouse and entered the city on 13 September, 1217. Most of the inhabitants welcomed it enthusiastically; the small French garrison had to take refuge in the Château Narbonnais, the strongly fortified residence of the count. Simon's brother and son managed to lead some reinforcements into the castle, but the garrison was still too small to think of retaking the town.

Raymond VI, quite sensibly, made no effort to take the Château Narbonnais. Toulouse was still an open city; the essential tasks were to make it defensible and to recruit enough troops to man a long perimeter. Raymond was remarkably successful in both jobs. Everyone in the city, high or low, rich or poor, man or woman, worked feverishly to erect a line of fortifications around the community. As a chronicler says: "Everyone began to rebuild the walls. Knights and burgesses, ladies and squires, boys and girls, great and small carried up the hewn stones singing ballads and songs." This was only common sense—no one had any illusions about what Simon would do if he broke into the city—but it was also a manifestation of Occitanian patriotism. For the same reasons men from all the southern provinces came to join Raymond's army. Many of them hoped to regain lost lands, and many of them feared Simon's vengeance if he were victorious, but there was an enthusiasm for Raymond's cause that transcended personal interests. For a brief moment Occitania was united as it had not been before and as it was never to be again. Toulouse was the symbol of resistance to French domination, and Raymond VI, in spite of his unheroic past, was the chosen leader in Occitania's fight for independence.

Simon, informed of the rebellion by his wife, left Provence at once and hurried toward Toulouse, picking up what troops he could on the way. He saw clearly that his best hope was to assault the city immediately, before its improvised fortifications could be strengthened. But a full-scale attack ended in a bloody repulse and Simon realized that he would have to mount a regular siege. Everything was against him. It was late in the year (October) and the winter rains would soon begin; Toulouse was far too large a city to be surrounded by Simon's army, and reinforcements and provisions could enter freely; and even if the city were surrounded the Garonne flowed past one side so that there could be no shortage of water or of supplies brought in by boat. Simon did what he could. He had no trouble in persuading Honorius III to renew the call for a Crusade, but crusaders could not be expected to arrive before spring. He tried to take the suburb of St. Cyprien that controlled the ends of the two bridges leading into the city. Possession of St. Cyprien would have made it easier for Simon to control river traffic and to block some supplies entering Toulouse, though it probably would not have given him a decisive advantage. But the attack on St. Cyprien failed, and, as the weather worsened, it became more difficult to mount any operations. Morale in Toulouse remained high, but it began to sink among the besiegers.

With the coming of the spring of 1218, both sides received reinforcements. Two groups of crusaders joined Simon; Raymond VII brought in troops to aid his father. The latter set off a fresh burst of enthusiasm. "When the people of the town saw the banners, they rushed toward the count as if he had risen from the dead. And when the count entered through the vaulted gates the people came to him, great and small, barons and ladies, women and men. They fell on their knees and kissed his clothes, his feet, his legs, his arms, and his fingers. It was with tears of joy that he was received . . . and the count in great happiness dismounted at the monastery of St. Sernin,[3] the powerful and kindly saint, who never wanted Frenchmen around him. Trumpets and horns sounded, the flag-bearers shouted their war-cries, and the sound of bells filled the city."

With his fresh troops, Simon tried again to take St. Cyprien, but while his men gained a foothold several times, they never controlled the bridgeheads. Direct attacks on the fortifications of the city were repulsed, with heavy losses on both sides. Simon's followers had been spoiled by his habit of winning victories quickly; they grumbled about the tedium and the hardships of the siege; even the papal legate complained about the delay in taking Toulouse. Simon decided to try once more to break through the fortifications. He constructed a huge

---

[3] The largest and most magnificent church in Toulouse, where Raymond IV had taken the vow to go on the First Crusade.

"cat," a rolling wooden tower that could be pushed up to the main line of defense. Its base would fill the outer ditch; its upper stories would dominate all other defense works. The Toulousans realized the danger; as the tower approached their lines they concentrated all their stone-throwing machines on it and, on 25 June, sortied in force. There was a period of confused fighting, but, just as the sortie was finally flung back, a stone, flung from inside the city, struck Simon on the head. According to the Toulouse legend, the machine was operated by a crew of women. Whoever triggered the shot hit the mark squarely. Simon's skull was crushed and he died at once.

Simon was one of the greatest generals of the Middle Ages. Few other men accomplished as much with as small forces; few other men had his eye for an enemy weakness, his ability to make quick decisions, his courage and his tenacity. But while Simon was a great soldier, he was a mediocre politician. He had conquered a principality, but he had not created the institutions that would hold it together, nor the loyalties that would enable his son to continue his work. The political victory that established French rule on a firm basis was to be won by Louis VIII and Louis IX of France, not by the Montforts.

Simon's death marked the end of the first of the Albigensian Crusades, the one in which the leadership was provided by barons from the North of France. No one appeared who could take Simon's place. His eldest son, Amaury, succeeded him as count and as commander of the crusading army, but Amaury was simply a respectable young man with no particular gifts of leadership. He could do nothing to raise the spirits or strengthen the determination of his army. The siege was lifted in July, and all through the South men celebrated the triumph of Toulouse and the death of Simon.

Then the defections began. They were especially numerous around the edges of the old Montfort holdings; most of Agenais in the west and the city of Nîmes in the east recognized the Raymonds as their rulers; the count of Comminges drove the French garrison out of his county; the count of Foix raided the plains between the mountains and Toulouse. It was clear that Amaury could not stop these losses; it was equally clear that the only person who could was the king of France.

Appeals went once more to Paris, this time with a new inducement: the promise of financial support from the Church. Innocent III, the great innovator, had imposed the first income tax on the clergy—a tax of one fortieth of their revenues for aid to the Holy Land. As usual, the rate and the frequency of the tax went up; the Lateran Council of 1215 asked for one twentieth of revenues for each of three consecutive years. Now Honorius III promised Philip half of the twentieth paid by the French clergy if he would aid Amaury. This offer, plus a suggestion that the count of Champagne might be a good leader if Philip refused to act, persuaded the king that he must send his son south again. But Honorius had paid a greater price than he realized for his diplomatic victory. From this time on kings and princes demanded subsidies from the Church before they would fight to defend its policies. By the end of the century they were so accustomed to receiving clerical subsidies that they considered them part of their regular revenues and used them for purely secular purposes. Thus the income tax imposed on the clergy for the purpose of paying for Crusades became a tax levied on the clergy to pay for national wars.

Louis was reluctant to undertake the expedition, as even the pope realized. He was still annoyed by the bitter opposition of the Church to his attempted conquest of England, and by the financial penalties imposed on him when he was absolved from the excommunication he had incurred. The fact that Honorius offered to let him use this money for a Crusade against the Raymonds merely reminded him of his humiliation. Yet, in the conditions of 1218–1219, it would have been unwise to refuse to go; the dynasty needed to preserve its old alliance with the Church. So Louis agreed to lead a Crusade, but his heart was not in it; what little he did helped him and his family more than it did Amaury de Montfort.

Louis set out in May 1219 and took the western road through Poitou rather than the usual crusaders' route down the Saône and the Rhône. Since Poitou was still disputed between the kings of England and France, the presence of a large French army in the county was bound to encourage the supporters of Philip Augustus. After passing through Poitou, Louis joined Amaury at the siege of Marmande, a small town on the border between Agenais and the English holdings around Bordeaux. Faced with far stronger forces, the garrison of the town surrendered. The lives of the commander and his knights were spared; everyone else in the town was massacred. Even chroniclers used to years of violence were struck by the ferocity and the blood-lust of the victors; nothing quite so brutal had been seen since the slaughter at Béziers. The southern chroniclers are full of gory details: "Limbs and bodies, flesh and blood, broken fragments of human organs lay in every open place. The ground, the streets, the shore were red with blood. No one was left alive, man or woman, young or old." A northern writer said tersely that "they killed all the townsmen with their wives and children, everyone, up to the number of five thousand." This was a little less than the toll at Béziers, but only because Marmande was a smaller town.

It is difficult to find a reason for the massacre at Marmande. There were heretics there, but it was not an important town nor did it occupy a strategic position. It had been one of the first places to defect after the death of Simon, and it is probable that the Montforts wanted to destroy it as a warning to others. But Louis could have restrained the Montforts and the decision to slaughter the inhabitants of the town was taken in cold blood in a council at which he was present. Louis was seldom guilty of senseless cruelty; he may have hoped to terrify other towns as Simon had terrified them by the sack of Béziers. But the people who were terrified by the fate of Marmande were the burgesses of English-held towns, not the men of Toulouse. Louis may have hoped for this result; certainly he met little opposition a few years later in his operations in Poitou and along the border of Aquitaine.

After Marmande, Louis laid siege to Toulouse. This was hardly a serious affair; he did not push home his attacks and his barons and knights showed no desire to die for the Montforts. Toulouse was stronger than ever; the citizens were exalted by their previous success. Only a determined and patient army willing to camp outside the walls for months or years could have hoped to take the town. Neither Louis nor his army were patient or determined; after about six weeks they raised the siege and went home.

This "miserable setback" (to quote Honorius III) practically ended Amaury's chances of holding on to his father's conquests. He had already been defeated by Raymond VII in a brisk little battle at Baziège (just before the siege of Marmande); he had now failed to retake his capital city even with the aid of a crusading army led by the heir to the throne. If he could neither win battles in the open country nor take walled towns, Amaury was not to be feared. This obvious conclusion was reached by both friend and foe. Most of Amaury's soldiers left him; he had no money with which to hire mercenaries, and few crusaders came to help him. Town after town, castle after castle slipped out of his grasp. Amaury did not give up at once; he had some of his father's tenacity, if little of his ability. When Raymond VII took Castelnaudary, Amaury still had

strength enough to mount a long siege of the town (July 1220–
March 1221). But the place was well supplied and the besiegers were harassed by frequent sorties. Guy de Montfort,
younger brother of Amaury, was killed in one of these clashes
—a serious loss, for he was probably the better fighter of the
two. The siege had to be abandoned, and after this failure
Amaury could no longer react with any vigor. Raymond VII
and his faithful supporter, the count of Foix, advanced steadily
and methodically. They ran no unnecessary risks; they were
careful to avoid places like Carcassonne, where the remaining
Montfort strength was concentrated, or Narbonne, where old
archbishop Arnaud Amaury was still defying his enemies. But,
except for these remnants of Simon's original conquests, by
1222 Raymond VII had regained everything that had been lost
by his father.

It was in 1222 that Raymond VI died. He might have died
happy, if the hostility of the Church had not pursued him to
the grave and beyond. Because he had never been fully absolved—though he sought absolution repeatedly—he was denied the last sacraments and burial in consecrated ground. This
seemed a harsh judgment on a man who, if never absolved,
had never been condemned—the sort of judgment that was
later to emanate from the Inquisition, where men were punished on mere suspicion of heresy. It seemed a harsh judgment
to Raymond VII, one of whose most admirable traits was his
devotion to his father. He spent the rest of his life trying to

secure Christian burial for the old count; his opponents took advantage of this filial piety by raising vain hopes that if young Raymond were only a little more docile the ban on his father might be lifted.

In 1223 Raymond Roger of Foix died in his turn. He had been the best and most persistent fighter against the Montforts, but Amaury gained nothing by his death. His heir, Roger Bernard, was just as capable, just as loyal to the count of Toulouse, and just as determined to drive the Montforts from the land.

Even before the death of the counts Amaury had realized that his cause was lost. He had offered his lands to the king, but Philip Augustus, as he became older and feebler, was more than ever opposed to southern involvements. Amaury had tried to borrow money, but he could offer no good security. His little lordship of Montfort in the North was of small value, and no one believed that he could retain his southern counties. Honorius III wrote indignant letters on his behalf, but the Occitanians were not impressed by papal denunciations and the French sent neither men nor money in response to papal pleas. The war dwindled into petty skirmishes and ended on 16 January, 1224, in a face-saving truce. Amaury was to seek advice from his friends in the North and try to reconcile the counts of Toulouse and Foix with the Church; meanwhile, his few remaining vassals and garrisons were to be unharmed. Actually, Amaury was abandoning the South to Raymond VII in return for an honorable exit. Montfort fortunes had sunk so low that Amaury could not even complete his journey without leaving his uncle as a pledge for his debts with some merchants of Amiens. There could be no thought of his return.

Meanwhile Raymond VII occupied Carcassonne and Béziers without resistance. It is significant that he gave them at once as fiefs to Raymond Trencavel, son of the viscount Raymond Roger who had died in the prisons of Simon de Montfort fifteen years earlier. If any Occitanian family had aided and protected heretics it was the Trencavel; now a Trencavel was once more viscount of Béziers and Carcassonne. The Occitanian counterattack had been completely successful. The dispossessed, from Raymond VII down to petty barons, were back in their old places; no Frenchman held a fief of any importance. The heretics were also back in their old places, but the lords of Occitania worried less about this fact than they should have. For the moment, it looked as if the Albigensian Crusades had been a complete failure.

VIII

THE KING'S CRUSADE
AND THE
FINAL SETTLEMENT

The popes were by no means committed to keeping the Montforts in power in Toulouse; Innocent III had had his doubts
about dispossessing Raymond VI, and Honorius III was at
first not unfriendly to Raymond VII. But they were committed to wiping out heresy, and now that the Montfort principality was collapsing, the heretics were once more becoming
conspicuous. A political solution that left the heretics un-
troubled was unacceptable, and Honorius III concluded that
only a Crusade or the threat of a Crusade would force Raymond VII and his allies into making a serious effort to eradi-
cate heresy. If a new Crusade were necessary it was perfectly
apparent that only one person could lead it—the king of
France.

As it happened, 1223 and 1224 were bad years in which
to persuade a king of France to go on Crusade. During the
first half of 1223 Philip Augustus was dying; during the second
half of the year Louis VIII was making the adjustments neces-

sary at the beginning of any new reign. Most of 1224 was spent on a problem that had long concerned Louis, the unsettled condition of Poitou. During a generation of Anglo-French hostilities the barons of Poitou had changed sides repeatedly, but on the whole they had been opposed to the assertion of French royal authority in the county. Louis broke their resistance; after 1224 he was in firm control of Poitou proper. But the border zones and the dependencies of Poitou ran into Occitania, and these outlying districts were precisely the areas where boundaries were uncertain and the king's authority still unsure. Thus, only after the conquest of Poitou was Louis free to undertake an expedition to the South, and the conquest gave him an additional reason for finding such an expedition desirable.

Negotiations between Louis VIII and Honorius III had begun early in 1224, but neither king nor pope seemed to be eager to push them to a successful conclusion. Louis posed very stiff conditions for his participation in a Crusade: The Church was to meet most of his expenses; he was to be free to go and come as he chose; he could annex any lands overrun by his army. In short, if he could get Toulouse and Carcassonne-Béziers quickly and cheaply, he would act, but he was not going to spend his life fighting in the South as Simon de Montfort had done. The bluntness of the demands was perhaps more annoying than their content, and it is possible that Louis meant to be annoying. He had, as we have seen, good reasons in 1224 for wishing to defer a Crusade; later on, when he really wanted to go, he was more diplomatic in framing his demands.

As for Honorius III, he seems to have been a little worried by Louis' announcement that if he went south he would take over the old Montfort possessions. Like Innocent III, Honorius was not sure that he wanted a strong ruler in Occitania; like Innocent III, he dreamed of installing a prince in Toulouse or Carcassonne who would be a dutiful vassal of the Holy See; like Innocent III, he wondered for a few months if the head of the old ruling family of Toulouse might not play this role. Like Innocent again, he would have preferred to reserve the king of France for a great Crusade to recover Jerusalem—and it is a fact that the Albigensian Crusades and their aftermath kept the kings of France from participating in overseas Crusades for three decades.

Whatever his reasons, Honorius refused to accept Louis' proposals. He suggested instead that the king frighten Raymond VII into making his peace with the Church, and that then some settlement be worked out that would indemnify Amaury de Montfort while leaving Raymond in possession of most of his family lands.

The idea of acting as the pope's bogeyman, all for the profit of Raymond and Amaury, infuriated Louis VIII. He abruptly ended negotiations with Honorius and went off to Poitou. But whether he wished it or not, Louis' presence with strong forces on the borders of Occitania had exactly the effect that the pope desired. Raymond was terrified and did his best to satisfy the demands of the Church; Honorius was free to explore the possibilities of a reconciliation with the young count.

There is no reason to suppose that Honorius was acting in bad faith, but an organization like the medieval Church develops its own momentum which an individual, even a pope, finds hard to stop. The negotiations with Raymond VII followed almost exactly the pattern of those with Raymond VI; in spite of some early encouragement from the pope, in the end the count found it impossible to convince legates, councils, and southern bishops of his sincerity. It is difficult to see what more Raymond VII could have done than he did. He promised to punish and expel heretics from his lands, to redress all wrongs that he had done to southern churches, and to pay a large sum to Amaury de Montfort to quiet his claims. These were more than empty promises; Raymond returned the city of Agde to its bishop and indemnified other prelates whom he had injured. He probably intended to put some pressure on the heretics, both because he had less sympathy with them than his father had had, and because he saw that it was a political necessity. How far he would have gone in persecuting his own subjects is another matter. Perhaps his opponents were right in arguing that he would never have eliminated heresy if left to his own devices, but he was not given a chance to prove his good faith. He spent most of the second half of 1224 in negotiating with the archbishop of Narbonne (our old friend Arnaud Amaury) and other prelates; he promised to obey any orders given by the pope; he sent an embassy to Rome to seek terms for his reconciliation with the Church. All his efforts were useless. No definite agreement could be reached with the archbishop of Narbonne and in December Raymond's embassy returned from Rome empty-handed. It seems clear that by the end of 1224 Honorius had turned against Raymond.

We can only speculate about the reasons for this decision. The Montforts still had influence in Rome, and Amaury's uncle was present in the city as a member of a French delegation just at the time that Raymond's envoys were dismissed without an answer. It is true that the French mission was concerned primarily with Anglo-French relations, but it is hard to believe that a Montfort found no opportunity to remind pope and cardinals of the heroism and sufferings of Simon. It is possible that the promise of the emperor Frederick II to carry out an overseas Crusade entirely with his own resources made Honorius less reluctant to use the king of France against the Occitanians. But the simplest explanation is also the most likely. The head of any centralized organization has to rely on the advice of experts who know local conditions. The experts— the bishops and abbots of Occitania—were almost unanimously opposed to Raymond VII. They had not trusted the father and they would not trust the son. They were convinced that a strong French presence was necessary to preserve the rights of their churches and to crush heresy. Their arguments convinced the pope.

In the spring of 1225 Honorius sent Romanus, cardinal of Sant' Angelo, as legate to France. Romanus belonged to the great Roman family of the Frangipani; his self-confidence and his very real ability soon gave him a wide degree of influence over the king. But his importance should not be exaggerated; Honorius had already decided to ask Louis to lead a new Crusade and Louis had almost certainly decided that, sooner or later, he must accept the papal offer. The legate's real contribution was in arranging the details of an agreement between pope and king and in preventing the friction that had arisen in 1224. He also had the task of stage-managing a council of French prelates that would condemn Raymond VII and thus justify Louis' attack.

Romanus did both jobs very skillfully. After some months of preparation a council of the French clergy met on 30 November, 1226, at Bourges. Amaury de Montfort and Raymond VII presented their cases, but since the king was deliberately absent the council could decide only the strictly religious question of Raymond's request to be reconciled to the Church.[1] The result could never have been in doubt, but Romanus took no chances. He asked for written opinions from the prelates, forbade any discussion of the case, and sent Raymond away

---

[1] According to a well-informed witness, at one point Amaury challenged Raymond to accept the judgment of the French court of peers. Raymond refused; there might have been some interesting arguments if he had accepted. Raymond had a better case in feudal law than he had in canon law; there could be no doubt that he had been excommunicated.

without revealing the vote. After Raymond's departure the legate announced that the council had refused to absolve him because "he had not made satisfactory promises to obey the orders of the Church"!

This was an astounding conclusion, but it was necessary in order to validate the next steps. At a meeting with the king and his barons in January 1226 Romanus renewed the excommunication of Raymond VII and his vassals, the count of Foix and the viscount of Béziers. Amaury de Montfort definitively ceded his claims to the king. The legate confirmed the king's right to all of Raymond's lands and asked the king to lead a Crusade. The barons supported the request, and the king took the Cross on 30 January, 1226.

Most of Louis' demands of 1224 were satisfied by decisions taken at this meeting or by later acts of the legate. Thus, the king obtained what he wanted without forcing the pope to make public concessions. For example, the king's right to quit the Crusade whenever he chose was guaranteed by the legate and sixteen French bishops. It was the legate who promised the king a tenth of ecclesiastical revenues of the French clergy for five years (a much larger sum than Louis had asked in 1224).[2] And it was the legate who preached the Crusade—and who collected money from those who wished to redeem their vows.

---

[2] Romanus claimed that the tenth had been granted by the council at Bourges; as Petit-Dutaillis showed long ago, this is unlikely. We do not know how long the French clergy paid the tenth; certainly not for five years, since collections ceased soon after the king's death in November 1226.

No earlier Crusade had been so well financed, and this alone would have produced a large army. In addition, Louis demanded full military service from his vassals; this was a war to recover royal lands (the Montfort cession) as well as a Crusade. His summons increased the size of both the army and the war chest, since he took fines from those who could not or would not serve. But the summons also added a disaffected element to the king's forces. The chroniclers report that many men resented being forced to fight against Raymond, and certainly there were occasions when the army showed some lack of enthusiasm for its work.

The army assembled at Bourges in May 1226. There is no possible way to estimate its numbers, but it was surely the largest force ever sent against the southerners. Its mere size terrified the Occitanians. Even before it began to move, some lords made their submission to the king; as it advanced down the Rhône more and more promises of obedience came in. It is especially noteworthy that the towns, which had been the first to defy Simon, feared to oppose Louis VIII. From Béziers and Carcassonne through Nîmes and Beaucaire over to Marseilles the towns abandoned Raymond and asked for the protection and clemency of the king. Of the larger towns Toulouse alone did not panic; it was still loyal to its old dynasty, still ready to fight against French domination. A few smaller places such as Agen followed the lead of Toulouse and a number of lords from the western part of Occitania (notably the count of Foix) promised their support to Raymond. But the count was much weaker than he had been at the time of the great siege of Toulouse, much weaker than he had been when he opposed Louis in 1219. It says much for his courage that he did not give up hope, but stood ready to meet the attack of an apparently irresistible army.

As it happened, the one important military action of the Crusade of 1226 took place far from Toulouse and more or less by accident. Louis VIII planned to cross the Rhône on the bridge at Avignon and had reached an agreement with the town government that guaranteed him free passage. But Avignon was one of the great cities of Occitania, as proud of its independence as Marseilles, as confident in its strength as Toulouse. It had some affection for Raymond VII, who, as marquis of Provence, was one of its suzerains, and it had aided him in the campaign against Beaucaire. It had well-founded fears of French domination. Avignon, after all, was not part of the kingdom of France; it was a city of the Holy Roman Empire, and it was much to its advantage to remain a city of the Empire. The emperor had almost no authority in Provence and absolutely no authority in Avignon; Raymond VII had only a vague claim to respect. Avignon was much more like an Italian city-state than a French municipality; its institutions resembled those of Bologna rather than those of Paris. The presence of a large French army in the neighborhood of what was virtually an independent republic was bound to cause fear.

The idea of letting this army march through the streets of the city became more and more repugnant as the date of the king's entry approached. The Avignonese began to seek ways to evade their agreement. They hit on the device of building a temporary wooden bridge over the Rhône outside the walls of the town. The vanguard of the crusaders crossed the river on this bridge without protesting, but Louis VIII, when he arrived, categorically refused to use it. He had been promised access to the great stone bridge that led from the heart of the city to the other side of the Rhône and he insisted on the fulfillment of the promise.

Louis may have feared, with reason, that the new bridge was not very substantial. But it seems likely that he was more worried about his prestige than about possible dangers to his army. Like most men of his class, he looked down on the bourgeoisie; who were these upstarts to tell the heir of Charlemagne where he could or could not go! In addition, the legate must have had a poor opinion of the Avignonese—they had been under an interdict for refusing to obey the pope—and he had great influence on the king. But the basic problem was that the towns formed the hard core of Occitanian resistance. If one town could bar the king and his troops from entering its gates, then so could the others, and if the army could not enter the towns then the whole expedition would be useless. Louis did not want to fight at Avignon; he tried repeatedly to persuade the burghers to admit him, and for a moment it seemed that he had succeeded. But when he sent a party forward to enter the town it found the gates barred. Louis was furious; he vowed not to leave his camp until Avignon was taken. The legate denounced the citizens as heretics and protectors of heretics. On 10 June, 1226, the siege of Avignon began.

Of the many sieges that marked the Albigensian Crusades, that of Avignon was the least dramatic. The town walls were so strong that direct assaults were practically impossible; the besieging army was so strong that sorties were also nearly impossible. Each side had to try to surpass the other in endurance and each side suffered from playing the waiting game. Avignon could not be cut off entirely from outside supplies, but Louis had enough men to patrol the Rhône as well as to block the land approaches, and the city experienced some shortages of food. Raymond's supporters could not risk a direct attack on the French but they could make foraging difficult and dangerous and the crusaders also ran short of food. Summer heat and lack of sanitation encouraged the spread of disease among the besiegers; it is possible that the king himself became infected. Some barons grumbled at the length of the siege; the count of Champagne went home after serving the minimum of forty days required by feudal custom. Discontent among his men probably led Louis to mount a full-scale assault against the city early in August, but the attack was a complete failure and the siege continued.

By the end of August both sides were weary enough to

compromise. Louis had used up almost all the good weather; if he did not leave soon he could not hope to attack Raymond and Toulouse, and if he stayed he would have to face the new hardships of winter cold and rain. The Avignonese were convinced that Louis would not leave without some satisfaction. And the siege was already hurting them physically and financially; in a few more months they would be ruined. So a surrender was arranged on fairly easy terms. The town paid an indemnity of 6000 marks (Toulouse in 1216 had paid 30,000), destroyed its walls, and gave hostages, but there was no killing and no looting. On 9 September, 1226, Louis VIII entered the town peacefully.

The fall of Avignon was a notable achievement; it established French rule permanently in the South. Nevertheless, the delay caused by the resistance of Avignon meant that Crusade could not be completely successful. Most of Occitania was even more terrified than it had been before; if Avignon, one of the strongest towns in the region, could not resist, who could? The rest of the marquisate of Provence surrendered to the pope and accepted French garrisons, and Louis met no resistance on his march toward Carcassonne. But the fall of Avignon had terrified only those who were already awed by the king of France; it had not shaken the determination of Raymond VII and the men of Toulouse. Louis could not rush headlong on such enemies; he had to leave garrisons and establish some rudimentary administration in the lands that submitted themselves to his rule. These operations took time, and further reduced the strength of an army that had suffered heavy losses during the siege of Avignon. Louis did not draw near Toulouse until the middle of October; by that time it was evident that neither the king nor his soldiers were in any condition to attack the defiant city. Louis decided to return home and to drive Raymond from Toulouse in the following year. But the king was already ill, and the illness soon became mortal. Louis VIII died on 8 November, 1226, in the little town of Montpensier in Auvergne.

Raymond VII continued the war for two more years, but he was unable to make any significant gains. On the other hand, the new king, Louis IX (later, St. Louis) was a child, and his mother, Blanche of Castille, who acted as regent, was disliked by many northern barons. She was a woman and a foreigner; she was trying to maintain the strong government that her father-in-law had founded and that her husband had preserved. The barons wanted to regain some of their lost independence; Blanche had to face a long series of conspiracies and rebellions. In these circumstances, there could be no thought of renewing the Crusade. The most that Blanche could do was to maintain a garrison in the South strong enough to hold Raymond in check.

Thus, a situation which Louis VIII had considered only temporary began to take on attributes of permanence. Raymond held Toulouse and lands north of Toulouse; he could be driven out only at the cost of bloody fighting. The king held all of the old Trencavel lands—Albi, Carcassonne, Béziers—and everything east of the Trencavel viscounty to Beaucaire on the Rhône. Raymond had not been able to reconquer these lands while the king was a minor and while the regent was plagued with rebellions. It seemed unlikely that he could do better when Louis IX came of age. The Occitanians had not rallied to him after the death of Louis VIII as they had after the death of Simon de Montfort; they were tired of war and they knew the difference between resisting the Montforts and resisting the Capetians. During 1227 and 1228 many men began to think that it might be sensible to establish a permanent peace on the basis of existing boundaries. The regent and Raymond agreed to explore these possibilities, and a conference at Meaux, December 1228–January 1229, worked out a definite agreement. The peace was ratified at Paris on 12 April, 1229.

The terms of the treaty were harsh, but Raymond VII gained two things that had always been denied his father—reconciliation with the Church and recognition as count of Toulouse. The reconciliation involved a public act of penitence and, what was more important, a promise to hunt out and punish heretics. Raymond had to offer a reward of two marks (reduced after two years to one mark) to anyone who captured a heretic. The Church was to receive 14,000 marks in indemnities. Raymond also had to promise to pay 4000 marks for the salaries of professors of theology, canon law, and arts who were to come to Toulouse—this was an attempt to establish a center of orthodoxy in the heart of heretical lands, and led, in the end, to the foundation of the University of Toulouse. The price for his recognition as count of Toulouse (including Agenais, Rouergue, and parts of Albigeois and Quercy) was the marriage of his daughter to the king's brother, Alphonse. Jeanne of Toulouse was at the moment Raymond's only child, but the treaty provided that even if Raymond had other offspring she was to be the sole heir. The county of Toulouse was to go, on Raymond's death, to Jeanne and Alphonse and their children; if they were childless, it was to revert to the crown.

Some historians have wondered why Raymond agreed to a treaty that led to the extinction of the House of Toulouse. But this is arguing from hindsight; in 1229 no one could have foreseen that Raymond would have no more children and that the marriage of Jeanne and Alphonse would be sterile. If Raymond had had a son, he would certainly have received some of the family inheritance and might have claimed it all. As Raymond's own case demonstrated, there was a strong prejudice against ignoring the rights of a legitimate heir; solemn rulings of kings and popes had not prevented him from recovering Toulouse. If Jeanne had had a child she would have started a new dynasty that, in two or three generations, might have forgotten its obligations to its distant cousins in Paris and renewed the independent traditions of the Raymonds. Moreover, Raymond knew from past experience that treaties were not immutable and that there might be revisions in his favor. On one occasion such a revision actually took place: The treaty had confirmed papal possession of the marquisate of Provence but in 1234 the pope returned the marquisate to Raymond. In short, Raymond suffered no immediate territorial losses by the agreement of 1229, and he could hope that with good luck and changes in the political climate some of the unfavorable clauses would never take effect.

More important than the contingencies affecting Raymond's lands was the consolidation of the Capetian position in the South. The king was now in undisputed possession of a block of territory running from Gascony to Provence, garrisoned by his men and governed by his officials. Towns and barons could not resist royal power; the few uprisings that occurred were easily suppressed. Even the church lost some of the autonomy that it had enjoyed under the Montforts. Since the king could not be a vassal, fiefs that had been held of bishops and abbots by the Montforts or their predecessors were merged into the royal domain. The prelates were given lands of equal value in exchange, but these lands were usually located in places of less strategic importance and were often too scattered to form the nucleus of a powerful lordship. The bishops were forced to swear fealty to the king; this imposed very real obligations on them, even, according to some royal officials, the obligation of rendering military service. In the end, many southern prelates found it advisable to share their rights of government with the king. Thus, the royal government could now act directly in an area where it had long had no influence; it could put pressure on Raymond from the South as well as the North. Even if Raymond had had a son and even if the son had succeeded in inheriting most of his father's lands, the new count of Toulouse could not have been as independent as his twelfth century predecessors. The dominant power in Occitania was now the king of France.

The events of the next twenty years only served to confirm the fact that a decisive shift in the balance of power had taken place. There was real resentment against the arrogance and corruption of French officials in the districts held by the king. There was strong opposition to the Inquisition, a new institution devised by the Church to ferret out heretics. Yet there were only two half-hearted revolts during the last years of the old Toulousan dynasty. In 1240 the Trencavel viscount made one last effort to regain the family lands. He threatened Carcassonne for a few days, but was driven off and made his peace with the king. Raymond VII did not support the Trencavel uprising, not because he was loyal to the king but because the viscount had attacked prematurely. Raymond's own plans were more complicated; he was working out an alliance with Henry III of England and with the count of La Marche. This was poor material for a rebellion: Henry III was one of the least successful generals in the whole history of the English monarchy and the Lusignan counts of La Marche were notoriously unstable. Raymond's own subjects, even though they were irritated by the behavior of the Inquisition, were not eager for war. Only the heretics were willing to risk violence and they were more concerned with protecting themselves than in helping Raymond.

Raymond's rebellion began early in 1242. He had some success in conquering the region between Toulouse and Narbonne, but he did not coordinate his movements with those of his allies, and his allies showed no ability to act on their own. The count of La Marche did nothing and Henry III ran for Bordeaux as soon as he made contact with the army of Louis IX. Meanwhile, Raymond's life was complicated by the massacre of a group of Inquisitors at Avignonet, a small town southeast of Toulouse. The actual murderers were heretics from the mountain fortress of Montségur, but one of Raymond's officials had helped plan the ambush, and the killings took place on Raymond's land. The count was promptly excommunicated and the possibility of a new Crusade must have entered the minds of some men. Raymond's vassals began to desert him, not least the count of Foix, who transferred his allegiance to Louis IX. Raymond realized that it was useless to continue the struggle and submitted to Louis IX. He was punished very lightly, perhaps because the king realized that he was no longer dangerous, perhaps because it was evident that the king's brother would soon inherit the county of Toulouse and there was no point in impairing the inheritance, perhaps because the royal government already had its hands full and wanted no new territories to administer. Whatever the reasoning, the decision proved correct. Raymond made no more trouble. He spent the few remaining years of his life in futile attempts to find a wife who might produce a male heir, and he persecuted heretics with enough zeal to keep in the good graces of the Church.

Meanwhile, the royal government determined to avenge the massacre at Avignonet by taking the stronghold of Montségur. This fortress was a refuge for heretics, especially for those of noble blood, and had become the administrative center of the Cathar Church. Perched on a peak in the Pyrenees, accessible only by a steep winding path, well stocked with provisions, Montségur seemed almost impregnable. Nevertheless, Hugh d'Arcis, the king's representative in Carcassonne, undertook the almost hopeless task. In his courage and tenacity he proved himself a worthy successor of Simon de Montfort. The siege lasted a year (March 1243–March 1244); Hugh had to keep his men in the field through the awful cold of a mountain winter. There was no spectacular fighting, but week by week the French army inched closer to the walls. The weary garrison finally surrendered; their lives were spared, but the "perfect" were given the usual choice of abjuring their faith or death by fire. Two hundred men and women joyfully entered the flames rather than betray their religion.

The fall of Montségur marked the end of all serious armed resistance by the heretics. A few police operations were still necessary, but no real army had to be used again to deal with heresy in the South. The loss of Montségur also weakened the structure of the Cathar Church. Deprived of a secure head-quarters, subject to steady pressure by secular authorities, Cathar leaders found it increasingly difficult to preserve their organization. They did not give up at once, but Catharism never recovered from the blow of 1244.

With all opposition broken, the French royal family was able to consolidate its position in the South without difficulty. When Raymond died in September 1249 his lands went to his daughter Jeanne and her husband, Alphonse of France, count of Poitiers. The new count and countess were absentee landlords in the most complete sense of the phrase. They made a solemn entry into Toulouse in 1251, but did not appear in the South again until 1270 on their way to the Crusade against Tunis. Alphonse governed the county from Paris, largely through French officials, and in complete harmony with the wishes of his brother, the king. When Alphonse and Jeanne died without heirs in 1271, on their return from the Crusade, the new king of France, Philip III, took over their lands without any difficulty. What had been no better than an outside chance in 1229 became a reality. All that Simon de Montfort had gained by years of fighting, all that Raymond VII had salvaged by his wars of reconquest was now part of the royal domain. As the great French historian Luchaire wrote in 1905: "Everyone, from Innocent III on, had worked, struggled, and suffered, without realizing it, for the benefit of the king of France."

IX

THE UNDERGROUND CHURCH AND THE INQUISITION

One reason for the compromise political settlement of 1229 was that the Crusades had done very little to solve the problem of heresy. A new Crusade seemed unlikely to improve the situation. The killing of heretics was a mere by-product of wars of conquest or reconquest. Sometimes a few hundred were caught and burned after a victorious siege, and certainly some of the soldiers slain fighting for southern lords were heretics or supporters of heretics. But it is likely that more Catholics than heretics were killed in the wars, and in any case the pacifist doctrines of both Cathars and Waldensians meant that the majority of the heretics and their sympathizers were never involved in combat. It could be argued that the Crusades were necessary to create a political climate in which heresy could be repressed; indeed, this was the basic justification for the Crusades from beginning to end. But by 1229 there were parts of Occitania that had been governed for twenty years by entirely orthodox rulers, and the heretics seemed more numerous than before. Narbonne offers a striking example of the problem. The city had never contained many heretics, it had never been accused of favoring heretics, and its archbishop for many years was Arnaud Amaury, the legate who had led the first Albigensian Crusade. Yet by 1229 (only four years after Arnaud Amaury's death) there were probably more heretics in Narbonne than in 1209. There were obvious advantages to living in a peaceful city under the protection of a powerful prelate—as long as one was not caught. And this was precisely the difficulty—no one was very good at catching heretics. It is not surprising that laymen like Simon de Montfort were not skilled in detecting departures from orthodoxy, but it is surprising that the new bishops appointed by Innocent III were so unsuccessful. They were able to recognize Cathar leaders who held what were practically public services (though even some of these men escaped), but they seldom identified the followers and supporters of the leaders. The bishops were occupied with many problems—not the least of which were the Crusades—and apparently they did not have the time or the skill to organize a continuing and thorough search for heretics.

Gregory IX (1227–1241), who succeeded Honorius III as pope, gradually came to realize the futility of military operations. At first he urged the regent, Blanche of Castille, to continue the war against Raymond VII, but by 1229, when he allowed the legate Romanus to arrange the Treaty of Paris, he was obviously willing to consider other means of combatting heresy. The idea of making Raymond pay a bounty to anyone who denounced a heretic probably originated with Romanus; it was ingenious but we have no evidence to show that it was particularly successful. Romanus also held a council at Toulouse in November 1229 which tried to improve the technique of heresy-hunting. According to the canons of the council, every man over fourteen and every girl over twelve had to take an oath to seek out and denounce heretics. Old legislation requiring the bishops to appoint a priest and two laymen in each parish to investigate and report charges of heresy was renewed. Loss of office and property was the penalty for anyone who did not show sufficient zeal in supporting these investigations.

Romanus realized that the hunt for heretics had to be intensified, but he was not very successful in devising new methods for finding them. Most of the canons of the council of 1229 merely repeated the work of earlier councils, and the attempt to enlist the population in the task of discovering heretics proved a failure. Romanus was somewhat more successful in speeding up the process of convicting heretics. He forced those who had returned to Catholicism to denounce their former associates, and, contrary to the rules of canon law, he refused to let the accused know the names of their accusers. The bishops summoned to a council at Toulouse in 1229 were able, by following these methods, to investigate a mass of accusations; and the legate handed down sentences based on the reports of the prelates. But a council could not be called every time there was to be a heresy trial and not all legates were as energetic as Romanus. On the other hand, it was evident that the bishops, as individuals, were not doing a good job in discovering and convicting heretics.

Gregory IX saw, with increasing clarity, that heresy could be repressed only by establishing an institution designed specifically for this task and staffed with men who had expert knowledge of the problem. The experts were ready at hand: the friars of the Dominican Order. St. Dominic had begun his mission by attempting to convert the heretics of western Occitania; his first foundation, the nunnery of Prouille (1207), was created to receive women who had been reclaimed from Catharism. The Dominicans themselves were to be the Order of Preachers, men who would recall the ignorant, the careless, and the sinful to the true faith. St. Dominic's followers were trained in theology, so that they could not be deceived by the quibbles of heretics; they also had the practical experience of living in towns and cities among the poor and the disaffected. They knew more about heresy and more about the behavior of the masses than did most bishops. They were ideal instruments for Gregory's plans.

The pope began by giving extraordinary powers to repress heresy to agents sent to regions where the bishops were too busy or too careless to perform their duties. The first clear example of this practice was the mission of Conrad of Marburg in Germany in 1231. Conrad was not a Dominican (though the Dominicans were soon asked to assist him) and while he seriously abused his powers he did very nearly wipe out heresy in the Rhineland. Dominicans were used in Florence and in the Po valley; it also appears that the bishop of Toulouse and the archbishop of Narbonne relied on Dominicans to prosecute heretics. These preliminary experiments gave promising results; in 1233 Gregory IX decided to generalize his use of the preaching friars. He told the French bishops that they were overburdened with work and that he was sending the Dominicans to assist them in the task of eliminating heresy. The Dominican prior of Provence was asked to name specially qualified friars to act in the dioceses of Occitania, while the Dominican Robert le Bougre, a converted Cathar, was commissioned to act in the North.

One cannot say that the Inquisition was founded at any one moment, but these acts mark a turning point in papal policy. Before 1233 the bishops had the chief responsibility for discovering and investigating cases of heresy, even if they were assisted from time to time by agents designated by the pope. After 1233 the responsibility fell more and more on specially appointed inquisitors, usually drawn from the Dominican Order.[1] The bishops naturally resented this interference with their jurisdiction and tried to keep the inquisitors subject to their authority or even to prevent them from acting. But while the bishops gained some temporary victories, and some face-

---

[1] A good many Franciscans also were used, sometimes in conjunction with Dominicans, sometimes by themselves. In the latter case, the Franciscans were usually assigned to districts in which there were few heretics. Monks and cathedral clergy were also used occasionally.

saving forms of procedure, by the second half of the thirteenth century they had definitely lost control of heresy prosecutions in France. Bishops still acted occasionally on their own authority, and they were asked to give formal approval to acts of inquisitors, but the real work of discovering and trying heretics was performed by the Inquisition.

The organization of the Inquisition as a separate and clearly defined institution also took time; even the first stages were barely completed by the 1250's. But the basic procedures of the Inquisition appeared almost at once and its efficacy was proved long before it was institutionalized. Gregory IX had found the correct formula: The inquisitors were first to preach and to promise light penances to those who voluntarily confessed their errors; then they were to investigate carefully all charges against those who had not come forward. Since one of the essential signs of real repentance was to name everyone whom the penitent thought might be either a heretic or an associate of heretics, and since mere suspicion created such a presumption of guilt that those accused could clear themselves only by confession and revealing more names, it is easy to see how the inquisitors rapidly accumulated long lists of persons to be investigated. These carefully preserved lists were the real strength of the Inquisition. By checking one list against another, by patiently accumulating bits and pieces of evidence over many years, they were able to identify most of the heretics in their districts. Of course, they also listed thousands of people who had done nothing worse than talk to a heretic or dine in a heretic's house, but if the names of such small fry were written down very few of the big fish could hope to escape notice.

The penalties inflicted by the Inquisition were nicely calculated to produce a maximum number of denunciations. Those who confessed quickly and talked freely could gain absolution by giving alms and making one or two short pilgrimages. Those who resisted longer might have to wear a colored cross on their garments, a sign that exposed them to public contempt. Those who broke down only when threatened by death were imprisoned, often for life. It should be said that the prison was not very strict; usually it was an open, walled space in which prisoners could move around freely and where they could receive visits from their families. Nevertheless, since imprisonment meant forfeiture of property and inability to earn money, the economic consequences were severe. Finally, for those who relapsed into heresy after having been absolved and for those who refused to recant, the penalty was "relaxation to the secular arm." This was a hypocritical euphemism for the death sentence. The Church knew quite well that rulers in most countries where heresy was a problem had ordered that unrepentant heretics be burned at the stake; the Church had approved this legislation and would have attacked secular authorities who failed to inflict the death penalty. There was little danger of such leniency, both because lay rulers received the confiscated property of convicted heretics, and because no one wished to seem lukewarm in protecting the faith. However, by using the formula of "relaxation" the Church was able to follow the letter of the law which forbade clergymen to shed blood.

The threat of punishment was enough to make many of the accused confess at once; skillful interrogation by the Inquisitors led many more to admit their errors. We have lists of some of the questions that were asked, models used in training new inquisitors. Some heretics were very clever in evading incriminating answers; they would say that they were good Christians (which in their own sense they were), and that they believed all that they ought to believe, or all that was taught by "good masters." They could be tripped up by asking them questions about the Creation, or about the real presence of the body and blood of Jesus in the Communion wafer, or by demanding that they take an oath (forbidden by the Cathar religion). If these measures failed, the accused were subjected to psychological and physical pressure—repeated interrogation, imprisonment in dark and narrow cells, and, as a last resort, torture. In these circumstances it is not surprising that most prisoners renounced whatever errors they held and revealed the names of all their friends and associates. What is surprising is that hundreds held out to the end and went to the stake without betraying their fellows or renouncing their faith.

Neither the efficacy nor the evil consequences of the Inquisition should be measured by the number of death sentences it imposed. For the inquisitors a death sentence was a confession of failure. It meant that they had been unable to save an immortal soul; it also meant that they had been unable to acquire information about other heretics. Even the "perfect," the leaders of the Cathars, were let off with light sentences if they cooperated with the Inquisition, and simple believers were seldom put to death. After the Inquisition had made a few spectacular examples, such as the burning of 210 heretics at Moissac in 1234, and after the first wave of resistance had been broken, death sentences became comparatively rare. Even relapsed heretics were sentenced simply to life imprisonment, unless there were aggravating circumstances.

The first effect of the Inquisition was to drive the heretical churches, and especially the Cathar Church, underground. Even after the Treaty of Paris many nobles and a considerable number of town officials had made no secret of their sympathy for or belief in Catharism. The "perfect" held meetings and recruited new members without much attempt at concealment. It was difficult to arrest nobles even when they were notorious supporters of heresy; it was difficult to operate in towns where the municipal government was openly hostile to the inquisitors. The Dominican convent at Narbonne was sacked in 1234; the Dominicans were expelled from Toulouse in 1235; two inquisitors were killed in a riot in the little town of Cordes in 1233. But the friars could count on the wholehearted support of the king of France and the forced support of Raymond of Toulouse who did not want to risk the loss of his county. The king's seneschals broke down all resistance to the inquisitors in the royal domain and Raymond, with less enthusiasm, made it possible for the Inquisition to function in Toulouse and the other towns in his county. Supported by secular authority, sustained by their own very real courage, and inspired by the memory of their founder, the inquisitors accomplished an unbelievable amount of work in less than five years. There were never very many inquisitors—often only two for several dioceses—but two energetic inquisitors could deal with thousands of cases in a single year. For example, two inquisitors working in Toulouse in 1246 condemned thirty-four heretics in a single day. They did not keep up quite so rapid a pace thereafter, but they averaged about twenty-five condemnations a month for the period for which we have a record. All of the condemned were sent to prison, except for six who escaped. When it is remembered that these same inquisitors were active in places other than Toulouse and that the record for Toulouse is incomplete, we can see how effective the Inquisition could be. By the 1240's, the Cathar Church was badly disorganized in many places. The "perfect" were in hiding or had fled to fortified refuges such as the castle of Montségur in the Pyrenees; the simple believers were cut off from their leaders and were demoralized by secret accusations. A certain amount of outward conformity had always been permitted to those who had not received the *consolamentum* (the laying on of hands that granted full membership in the Cathar faith); now this leniency had to be extended to the "perfect" themselves. There was a double danger here: Acts of outward conformity, repeated often enough, sometimes led to genuine conversion to Catholicism; and outward conformity often required revealing the names of suspected heretics. For example, Bernard Otto of Niort, one of the most powerful barons of the Toulouse region, was certainly a heretic and eventually became one of the "perfect." Yet Bernard Otto was able to convince many clergymen, including an archdeacon, that he was an orthodox Catholic, probably because he had betrayed a number of his fellow-Cathars. If such a man could not be relied on, what trust could be placed in weaker and poorer believers?

When the Cathar leaders went underground both they and their followers became more vulnerable. If any contacts between the "perfect" and the ordinary believers were to be preserved, a whole set of clandestine operations had to be organized. Meetings had to be arranged in woods or other secluded places; safe houses had to be found where the "perfect" could be lodged on their travels; food and money had to be collected for the support of the wanderers. One slip might lead to the discovery of a whole group of heretics. For example, a collector of food or money might be caught on his rounds. He would reveal the name of the messenger who was to carry the collection to the hidden leaders; the messenger would be forced to name the place of rendezvous; and at least some of those who appeared at the meeting-place could be pressured into giving the names of other heretics. As a result, the inquisitors would end up with a list of dozens, or even hundreds, of suspects. The "perfect" would have to flee; many of their most zealous assistants would be arrested; and the simple believers would be left without leadership or organization.

An example of these problems may be found in the confession of Guillaume Sicre, made to the Inquisition in Carcassonne in 1259. Guillaume acted as guide and host to several of the "perfect" for many years; his earliest activities go back to the 1240's. The "perfect" learned about local conditions and the names of believers from him. They frequently stayed in his house overnight, and counted on him to show them passes through the mountains. He carried messages, books, and sometimes money from one of the "perfect" to another. When Guillaume was captured he revealed a whole network of believers, safe houses, meeting places, and routes used by heretics in his part of the country. He incriminated about forty people; if only a few of these had talked as freely as he did, there would have been very few Cathars left in the region by the 1260's.

This vulnerability of the Cathar Church may explain why we hear more of the Waldensians after 1230. The inquisitors usually made a distinction between the two groups—a common phrase in their letters was "heretics [i.e., Cathars] and Waldensians"—and there are some indications that the number of Waldensians had increased by the middle of the century. The Waldensians did not need as integrated an ecclessiastical organization as did the Cathars, and their basic beliefs were very close to those of the Catholic Church. Thus, Waldensianism could survive the loss of its leaders more easily than Catharism could, and it was somewhat harder to detect an ordinary Waldensian believer than a Cathar. At the same time the Waldensians were just as opposed to the Roman Church as the Cathars, and like the Cathars they stressed poverty, abstinence, and withdrawal from worldly affairs. Hatred of priests and bishops, and admiration for men who led truly holy lives were the most attractive elements in heresy for the mass of the population, and the Waldensians could appeal to these sentiments as well as the Cathars. Thus it is likely that as educated leaders disappeared there was some confusion among the common people; men who had at first vaguely sympathized with Catharism later vaguely sympathized with Waldensianism.

The Inquisition had succeeded in making the heretics fear for their lives and freedom; perhaps as important was the fact that it made them fear for their pocketbooks as well. Economic pressure is often more effective than brute force. There is something heroic in defying an oppressor up to the point of death; there is nothing heroic in living for years in abject poverty. Moreover, a heretic might be quite willing to accept the risk of death for himself and yet hesitate to risk the ruin of his family. One of the most iniquitous and effective procedures of the Inquisition was to bring charges against the dead. It was easy to obtain accusations; a suspect asked to purge himself by revealing the names of other heretics often found it safer to name the dead than the living. A dead man could not contradict or take vengeance on his accuser, and it was almost impossible for any of his descendants to clear his name. If the charges were serious, the bones of the accused were removed from consecrated ground and burned, and his property confiscated. Thus, no heretic could be sure, even if he died in peace and good repute, that ten, twenty, or thirty years later his heirs might not be penalized. For example, in 1250 a witness accused seven men and women of being heretics in 1217; in 1250–1253, another witness, husband of a believer, mentioned nineteen people, of whom at least seven were dead, as heretics in the 1220's, and another group of eight, of whom six were surely dead, as heretics about 1212. It took three sessions, spread over three years, to obtain all these names, which shows how steadily the Inquisition applied its pressure. And if a heretic decided not to risk condemnation after death, but to seek reconciliation with the Church while still alive, the dangers were almost as great. Only by cooperating fully with the Inquisition could he avoid the sentences that led not only to death or life imprisonment but also to loss of property.

The fact that the property of convicted heretics went to the secular authorities increased the pressure. One reason for this practice was that the secular authorities had to meet the expenses of building and maintaining the prisons in which heretics were kept; another was that lay rulers did not like the Church to confiscate land, especially land that was held as a fief. The result was that the greater the number of severe sentences against heretics, the more the king profited. Such considerations had little effect on the pious Louis IX, who would have persecuted heretics in any case, but they had a considerable effect on his agents who wanted to demonstrate their ability by increasing their master's revenues. There were occasions when royal officials tried to increase the number of convictions, even if it required bypassing the regular procedures of the Inquisition.

These economic penalties encouraged the worst aspects of the Inquisition. It is unlikely that many innocent men were burned at the stake, since, as we have seen, it was much more to the interest of the inquisitors to secure promises of orthodox behavior than stubborn professions of heretical belief. Every chance was given to the accused to repent; only the truly convinced heretic risked death by fire. But, almost certainly, some innocent men went to prison, and even more certainly the innocent heirs of guiltless men suffered unjust penalties. One has only to read some of the confessions of those accused of heresy; they give precise details of meetings held in the distant past and incredibly long lists of the names of those who attended the meetings. Here there was room for cowardice and stupidity, spite and jealousy to do their worst work. Here was where the inquisitors' sincere conviction that anyone suspected of heresy could not be completely innocent had its gravest consequences. Conversely, the orthodox Catholics who asked again and again that the inquisitors be removed, or at least restrained, were not trying to save unrepentant heretics from the stake. They were trying to save their fellow-countrymen from prison and their property from confiscation. They were concerned about the demoralization of their society through secret and often unfounded accusations. They could see no end to the troubles caused by the Inquisition; now that its main work had been done they wished that it would go away.

The decade of the 1240's was crucial for the heretics, especially for the Cathars. At the beginning they could still hope that they might survive as an organized group and perhaps even regain some of their old strength; at the end they were profoundly discouraged. The revolt of Trencavel had failed; the revolt of Raymond VII had failed; the heretics' fortress of Montségur had been captured. Raymond VII had been badly frightened by his failure in 1242; instead of shutting his eyes to the presence of heretics in his lands he now persecuted them with a zeal that would have satisfied Simon de Montfort. In 1249 he burned 80 "believers" at Agen; if Raymond acted so harshly what could be expected from his heir, Alphonse of Poitiers? Added to all these misfortunes was the steady pressure of the Inquisition. By the 1250's Rainier Sacconi, a converted Cathar who had become an inquisitor, estimated that there were no more than two hundred of the "perfect" left in all of the South of France. This number of leaders, steadily reduced by further persecution, was too small to preserve the structure of the Cathar Church. Heresy persisted, but it was only a nuisance and no longer a danger.

Nevertheless, the Church did not relax its efforts. It had been too badly frightened to take any chances, and the few

Cathar leaders who remained were capable of blowing the scattered embers of heresy into a new conflagration if they were given a breathing space. Moreover, the Cathars were still strong in northern Italy and many of the "perfect" of Occitania had taken refuge with their co-religionists there. A small but persistent trickle of leaders seeped back into Occitania from Italy to comfort the faithful and to celebrate the rites of the Cathar Church. This trickle could have become a torrent if the Inquisition had not continued to function. Finally, the royal government profited from the work of the Inquisition— directly by receiving confiscated property, indirectly by seeing potential enemies imprisoned and their holdings transferred to friendly hands. Down to the 1290's the French government gave the Inquisition full support.

The task of the inquisitors, however, became much more difficult after the 1250's. Few prominent men, and almost no members of the nobility, joined the ranks of the heretics. The "perfect" were more skillful in concealing their activity. Living unostentatiously among the poor, some of them were able to carry on their ministry for ten or fifteen years without being caught. Meetings of middle and lower-class men were harder to detect than gatherings of the old sort that had been attended by members of baronial families and of the urban patriciate, especially as the heretics avoided large assemblies. It was during this period of a completely underground Cathar Church that the Inquisition perfected its technique of interrogation and began to use torture as a regular part of the procedure.

The courage and tenacity of the Cathars was amazing. Deprived of their leaders, without any hope of protection from secular authorities, in constant danger of betrayal by their neighbors, they still clung to their faith. Men made the long journey to Italy in order to be received into the ranks of the "perfect" and returned to spend the rest of their lives as missionaries. The faithful remained steadfast and discreet; very few of the "perfect" were betrayed by the rank and file. And even when, after years of effort, the Inquisition succeeded in catching some of the small group of leaders, the ordinary believers remained true to their faith.

At the very end of the century, under Philip the Fair (1285–1314), heresy remained a problem in the South. The accounts of his reign show that the prisons were still full—over 140 in the "wall" of Toulouse in 1293, 113 in the same jail in 1310. Confiscations still brought in thousands of pounds a year, 3164 *livres tournois* in the seneschalsy of Toulouse in 1311. Granting that the Inquisition was not always fair in its definition of heresy, it is still true that most of those convicted in the 1290's and early 1300's had some sympathy with Catharism.

It was under Philip the Fair that the Cathars had their last chance to save at least a fragment of their church. Philip quarreled bitterly with Pope Boniface VIII in 1297 and again in 1301; on the second occasion he drew up charges against the pope and sought to have him tried by a General Council.

At the same time Philip was engaged in a desperate war with Flanders, a war that led him to impose heavy taxes on his people. The whole kingdom was restive, and the South was especially unhappy because it had the Inquisition to worry about as well as high taxes. The Inquisition was increasingly annoying to the bourgeoisie, and Philip's agents warned him that several southern towns were on the edge of revolt. He responded by securing the recall of the chief inquisitor and by severely restricting the assistance given by royal officials to the Inquisition. This was a promising start, but the enemies of the Inquisition showed remarkably bad judgment in their dealings with the king. When Philip came to the South in the winter of 1303 to look the situation over and to try to calm down the country, he was irritated by the wild accusations and presumptuous familiarity of the anti-Inquisition group. The king's own confessor was charged with betraying royal secrets to the Flemings, and the leader of the malcontents of Carcassonne spoke to Philip as an equal. Now Philip was a good Catholic even if he disliked the pope, and he had a very strong sense of the dignity of the royal office. His real religion was the religion of monarchy; he would tolerate nothing that threatened the security of the throne. He seems to have decided that these wild men in the South deserved all that they were getting from the Inquisition and that they needed more rather than less discipline. His opinion was confirmed when the men of Carcassonne made a silly plan to bring in an Aragonese prince as their ruler. The leaders of the conspiracy were hanged, an enormous fine was imposed on Carcassonne, and all restrictions on the Inquisition were removed.

After this episode it did not matter when Pope Clement V (1305–1314) tried to moderate the zeal of the inquisitors. The pope made new rules in an attempt to protect the rights of the accused, and these rules were duly incorporated in canon law, but never really applied. The last push against heresy began— more methodical, more thorough, and more successful than ever before. The key figure was Bernard Gui, inquisitor at Toulouse from 1308 to 1323, and author of a manual for inquisitors that summed up all their carefully worked out techniques. Bernard himself condemned 636 persons—40 to the stake, about 300 to prison, the rest to lighter penalties. His colleagues were almost as active. The last traces of Catharism were wiped out and Waldensianism survived only in obscure Alpine valleys. By 1350 the long struggle, begun by St. Bernard two hundred years before, had finally ended.

＋I＋I＋I＋I＋I＋I＋I＋I＋I＋I＋I＋ X ＋I＋I＋I＋I＋I＋I＋I＋I＋I＋I＋I＋

LANGUEDOC

The steady decline of heresy in the South was accompanied by an even more rapid erosion of the political independence of the region. Raymond VII was kept under close control, but he did represent an old native dynasty and he did at times try to impose his own policies. However, when he was succeeded by his son-in-law, Alphonse of Poitiers, the county of Toulouse became, to all intents and purposes, a part of the royal domain. As we have seen, Alphonse did not even bother to live in his new fief; he ruled his lands from Paris, just as did his brother, the king. Alphonse imitated the royal administrative system; the only differences were that his agents were perhaps a little more efficient than those of his brother and that he imposed general taxes in his lands, an innovation that St. Louis, with his respect for old immunities, shunned. When Alphonse died, his lands were assimilated completely into the royal domain. All of Occitania between Aquitaine and Provence was now ruled, directly or indirectly, by the French crown.

The royal government worked steadily to reduce outside influences and to weaken nobles and ecclesiastics who still had some claims to autonomy. Treaties with the kings of Aragon (1258) and of England (1259) limited the ability of both rulers to interfere in southern affairs. The king of England became a vassal of the king of France, which meant that decisions of his courts in Aquitaine could be appealed to the Parlement of Paris. Appeals and threats of appeals kept him on the defensive for several generations. No exact boundary could be drawn between the duchy of Aquitaine and the French royal domain, but the fact that the status of many border regions was uncertain again had the effect of putting the English king on the defensive. The treaty with Aragon was neater and more conclusive. The king of Aragon renounced all his claims to lands north of the Pyrenees, except the lordship of Montpellier. This concession effectively ended Aragonese influence in Occitania. Montpellier went to a junior branch of the Aragonese royal family, but while it was at times a nuisance, it was not a power center. Philip the Fair acquired the rights of the bishop to parts of the town in 1293, and he and his successors put so much pressure on the Aragonese princes that they eventually ceded the rest of the town to the French.

As for lesser lords, administrative and judicial pressures combined with a few military demonstrations kept them in line. The count of Foix was the most obstreperous lord—and remained so for the rest of the Middle Ages. But while he had to be chastised every twenty or thirty years, he posed no real threat to royal power. The semi-independent bishops of the Massif Central were forced to share their rights of government with the king; for example, they established common courts to which officers were named by joint action of the king and the bishop. As for the towns, they retained most of their rights of local self-government but their interests were clearly subordinated to those of the kingdom as a whole. They paid heavy taxes, their external trade was regulated by royal officials, and they were bound by the decisions of courts and financial agencies in far-off Paris. Toulouse in 1200 had almost attained the status of a city-state; Toulouse in 1300 was simply a privileged municipality.

The net effect of all these changes was to separate the southern provinces ruled by the king of France from the rest of Occitania. Aquitaine, now reduced to the regions of Guienne and Gascony, went its own way. Provence, even though it fell into the hands of Charles of Anjou (a brother of Louis IX) and his descendants, also led a separate existence. But the five districts of Périgord–Quercy, Rouergue, Toulouse–Albi, Carcassonne–Béziers, and Beaucaire–Nîmes formed a solid block of royal territory that had many things in common—language, law and legal procedures, administrative systems, and social patterns. Men moved about freely in this region; the great cities of Toulouse and Montpellier attracted young men from rural areas, and in turn sent lawyers, administrative officials, and merchants throughout the countryside. On the other hand, very few men of the South moved to Paris, either as officials or as businessmen. The central government often treated the five southern districts as an administrative unit, and thus encouraged the people of those districts to think of themselves as forming a political entity. Thus, this section of Occitania acquired its own identity—the northerners began to call it Languedoc (as distinct from the French-speaking region of Languedoeil)[1] and the southerners accepted the designation. Eventually Languedoc was to have its own Estates, its own Parlement, and its own Chambre des Comptes.[2] But these institutions were a result, and not a cause, of the common interests and common way of life of the people of the region.

Languedoc was only a part of Occitania, but it was the largest and most vital part. In spite of the deaths and devastation caused by the Albigensian Crusades, in spite of the psychological and economic shocks caused by the tactics of the Inquisition, Languedoc remained prosperous and preserved its cultural identity. A large part of France's Mediterranean trade passed through the towns of Languedoc, and there was a considerable amount of industrial activity in the region. Until the

---

[1] In the South men said "oc" for "yes"; in the North they said "oeil" (later "oui"); hence the two names.

[2] As a result of the Hundred Years' War, and the temporary expansion of English-held lands, Perigord-Quercy and Rouergue were not included in such organizations as the Estates of Languedoc. Languedoc, officially, was composed only of Toulouse-Albi, Carcassonne-Béziers, and Beaucaire-Nîmes. But for our period (down to 1300) there was almost no distinction between the three southern and the two more northern districts, and generalizations made in the rest of the chapter apply to all five.

great medieval economic depression in the fourteenth century, Languedoc was one of the wealthiest parts of the kingdom. There were few cities in the North as large as Toulouse and Montpellier; there were few provinces—perhaps only Normandy—that contributed as much to the royal treasury. And, as long as the men of Languedoc paid their rents and taxes, and obeyed royal orders about suppression of heresy, regulation of trade, and currency controls, as long as they furnished soldiers for the royal army and accepted the decisions of royal courts, they were allowed a large degree of autonomy. They had their own language, their own law, and their own universities. No one tried to make them speak French or adopt French rules of procedure, contract, or inheritance. Simon de Montfort had tried to make Languedoc accept some of the principles of French feudal law—the royal officials who took over his conquests were wiser.

In fact, the great majority of the royal officials in Languedoc were natives of the region. The seneschals who represented the king in each district were usually northerners, though even this high post was occasionally held by southerners, such as the lord of Isle-Jourdain. But the castellans and viguiers who controlled the forts and administered the subdivisions of each seneschalsy were often southerners, and almost all the judges were drawn from the South. This last fact is not surprising; few Frenchmen had the education that would have enabled them to preside in courts that were heavily infiltrated with the procedures and the language of Roman law. And judges who

were born and educated in the South were determined to preserve southern law; they had absolutely no interest in trying
to bring it closer to the customary law of the Paris region.
While they were, on the whole, loyal servants of the king as
long as they were judges, few of them wanted to remain judges
very long. A judicial post gave prestige, but private practice
was vastly more remunerative. Most judges had spent a large
part of their lives defending the interests of bishops, barons,
and urban communities against the demands of the central
government. They had a certain sympathy for their fellow-
lawyers who were still engaged in this task. They would not
rule against the king, but they did tolerate an inordinate
amount of delaying tactics. As a result, attempts to assert or
increase royal rights in Languedoc usually led to lawsuits, and
the lawsuits might last for decades. If the central government
wanted quick results—or sometimes if it wanted any results—
it had to compromise. Thus the courts acted as a buffer between Paris and the South; they slowed the growth of royal
power to a pace that made it more or less tolerable for the
men of Languedoc.

In short, the historians who have asserted that the Albigensian Crusades impoverished Languedoc, destroyed its culture, and subjected it to the arbitrary rule of hated foreigners
have exaggerated the harm done by the wars. Even Béziers
recovered with remarkable rapidity from the massacre and
looting of 1209 and no other place suffered as much as Béziers.
The Inquisition was a great evil, but aside from the Inquisi-

tion, Languedoc was not treated badly during the latter half of the thirteenth century. The economic depression of the fourteenth century and the ravages of the Hundred Years' War did more physical damage to Languedoc than the Crusades did.

The real damage done by the Crusades was in the subtle and scarcely measurable areas of self-respect and cultural pride. In becoming a province of France, Languedoc became provincial. Occitan gradually became a dialect, instead of a national language. No one forced the young men of the South to learn French, but if they did not, they were thought of as country bumpkins. No one forbade poets to write verses in Occitan, but if they did, they remained in a literary backwater instead of being part of the mainstream of French writing. Languedoc was now part of a state in which the cultural traditions of the Paris area were supreme. It could either conform and lose its identity, or resist and become quaint. As is usual in human dilemmas, the people of Languedoc did a little of both, and, again as usual, they got the worst of both courses. They slowly learned to write and to speak French, but most of them did it badly—even today *"the* accent" (of Languedoc) is derided in Paris. They also preserved some of their old culture, but it had lost its vitality; after becoming quaint it became archaic and then artificial.

For much the same reasons, service in posts in the municipal or provincial governments was not completely satisfactory to the ablest men in Languedoc. It was not difficult to secure such appointments, but usually they led nowhere. Only a handful of southern ecclesiastics and lawyers were called to Paris to sit in royal councils and courts. Clear into the fourteenth century the kings retained a certain suspicion of men born in the South; they wanted the central government to be staffed by natives of the old royal domain—the Ile de France and surrounding areas. But if the southerner who entered public service could usually hope for nothing better than provincial office, then he was bound to think provincially. He became preoccupied with parochial interests, he could not understand or care about larger issues. The days when leaders of Occitania dealt on equal terms with popes and kings, when they played a role in all problems of European politics, were long since gone.

The one escape from the growing provincialism of Languedoc was to become more French than the French and more royalist than the king. Guillaume de Nogaret, who had been a judge in the South and then became one of the chief ministers of King Philip the Fair, offers one of the earliest and best examples of this attitude. When Nogaret became convinced that Pope Boniface VIII was trying to subvert the authority of the king, he simply took the pope prisoner, in order, as he said, "to defend my fatherland." To justify his position, Nogaret practically had to invent French patriotism. In excusing his actions, he spoke again and again of his *patria*—his fatherland—which was the kingdom of France.

The men of the North were bound together not only by

similarities in language and customs, but also by respect for the royal family. The Capetians, annointed by holy oil sent down from Heaven, healers of the sick, heirs of Charlemagne, were not always obeyed, but they were reverenced by the barons of the North. The king was their natural leader in times of great emergency; even the unscrupulous Plantagenets recognized his moral superiority. He was the natural heir of families that died out or forfeited their lands. But the traditions that clustered around Reims and St. Denis meant little to the men of the South. The religion of monarchy was a northern religion. Wholehearted acceptance of French domination in the South could not be based on personal loyalty to the king or on the myths of the Capetian house. What was needed was a realization that a new political entity had been created, that the old kingdom of France, a loose union of many countries under a common king, had been transformed into a single country with an increasingly powerful central government. By the end of the thirteenth century men who admired power and some degree of administrative efficiency could admire and respect the new kingdom of France. The kingdom could serve as a focus of loyalty for men who were not satisfied with provincial particularism and yet had no personal ties to the king.

It was easier for Nogaret (and some of his friends) to develop the concept of an all-embracing French patriotism because they had had thorough training in Roman law. Nogaret's idea of a fatherland was full of reminiscences of

Latin writers; he had even absorbed the idea that man's highest duty was to die for his fatherland. The common welfare demanded the preservation and the strengthening of the kingdom of France; no privileges were to be respected if they weakened the kingdom; anyone who threatened France was to be struck down, even if he were a pope. It is quite possible that some of Nogaret's ancestors had been heretics. In any case, like most southerners, he had little respect for the organized Church. He gave his full devotion to the French state, and as a result he attained a higher position than any other southerner was to hold for generations. For over ten years (1302–1313) Nogaret was one of the most influential ministers of Philip the Fair; he kept the king's confidence to the day of his death.

Nogaret, however, spoke for only a small number of southerners. Most of the men of Languedoc remained suspicious of the Paris government, uninterested in the welfare of France as a whole, and eager to preserve as much local autonomy as possible. They were slow to obey and quick to complain; even in time of war and invasion they paid their taxes grudgingly. They retained their old tendency to accept unorthodox beliefs; it has often been pointed out that the Huguenots were strong in many of the areas in which the Cathars had been strong four centuries before. (So, for that matter, were anti-clerical groups in the nineteenth century.) It took many hundreds of years to bring Languedoc fully into the French political and cultural community. The Albigensian Crusades were only the beginning of the long process through which Languedoc became, spiritually as well as politically, a part of the French state.

Meanwhile, western Europe had to deal with a number of problems created by the French conquest of Languedoc. France was now a Mediterranean power and even more closely allied to the papacy than it had been before. When the popes, following the dangerous precedent set by Innocent III, decided that they must control Sicily and Naples, they called on the French to drive out the anti-papal Hohenstaufen dynasty that ruled these lands. A Crusade was proclaimed, and a French prince was installed as king of southern Italy. This use of a Crusade for purely political purposes did much to discredit the Church and thus helped cause the spiritual malaise of the later Middle Ages. The error was compounded when another purely political Crusade, led by the king of France, was sent against Peter III of Aragon, who had intervened in Sicily. A papacy that took money from the faithful in order to play political games in Europe was not an institution that inspired respect.

The French were left with a tenuous hold on the southern part of the Italian peninsula, and a strong urge to intervene in Italian affairs. The wisest French rulers resisted this urge, but not all rulers were wise, and French armies invaded Italy in every century from the thirteenth through the nineteenth. And every French invasion involved France in papal affairs and the papacy in worldly politics. Neither party profited from these entanglements; usually both of them lost reputation and the support of other countries.

Thus the papacy, in annihilating its enemies, the heretics, had become dangerously dependent on its friends, the kings of France. The kings, in conquering Languedoc, had increased their power and also their temptations to misuse their power. The Albigensian Crusades made possible a series of errors by Roman pontiffs and French monarchs that contributed heavily to the crisis of late medieval civilization.

Epilogue

Carol Lansing

Since the 1971 publication of Joseph Strayer's *The Albigensian Crusades*, historians have rethought the problem of heresy in dramatic new ways. Strayer was a great political and institutional historian, and his study is a vivid and perceptive work of history. It recounts the political circumstances that surrounded the crusades, narrates the story of the crusades themselves, and suggests some of the long-term implications of the imposition of French royal control in the south. Strayer effectively placed the crusades at the center of the political transformations of the thirteenth century.

Yet Strayer did not explore the problem of heresy itself. Like other historians of his generation, he assumed that the crusades were a response to the scale of the threat posed by heresy in the south of France; that the Cathars were so successful in drawing converts that the Roman church had to respond. Walter Wakefield, the author of *Heresy, Crusade and Inquisition in Southern France, 1100–1250* (1974), another fine and carefully researched English language narrative of these events, similarly assumed that the persecution of the Cathars was a reaction to the threat they posed to the Roman church and the social order.

In the last two decades, historians have questioned this assumption and reopened the question of the nature of heresy. What, after all, does it mean to speak of a threat from heresy? Heresy is by definition relative: it exists only when it is created by orthodoxy. Only with the formulation of a body of orthodox beliefs is heresy possible, as deviation from those beliefs.[1] "Heretic" is the label used by a believer to define another person as deviant. People did not call themselves heretics. Indeed, in 1178, when the papal delegation sent to investigate heresy in Toulouse rode through the city's streets, the local populace called *them* heretics and apostates.

Heresy was defined in the Middle Ages as an opinion "chosen by human faculties, contrary to holy Scripture, openly taught, and pertinaciously defended."[2] Strayer set out the medieval justification for the persecution of heresy based on this definition: Only one reading of Scripture, that of the Roman church, could be true. Only the truths taught by the papacy and the church and the sacraments administered by the church could lead people to salvation—other faiths led souls to perdition. Heretics in fact were legally considered traitors; orthodoxy and authority were inseparable. Deviation from the faith taught by the church challenged the authority of the papacy—by extension the authority of Christ—and attacked the very foundation of Christian society. Thirteenth-century authorities thus believed that the persecution of heresy was essential to the protection of Christian society.

At the same time, heresy itself was a social construction.

176

As Robert Moore writes, heresy, like beauty, lies in the eye of the beholder. Medieval Europe was probably not a uniformly Christian society with a few deviant subgroups considered heretics. Instead, a variety of religious beliefs were common, and only in certain circumstances were some beliefs attacked as heresy. Many historians have come to the position that the "Christianization" of Europe was a glacial process.[3] Medieval Europeans were largely unable to read or write; their access to Christian teaching was the instruction of local clergy who had themselves been poorly taught. In many regions, local parish churches were established only in the eleventh and twelfth centuries. Requirements for parish priests were of necessity low: as late as the thirteenth century, they might have been expected only to know how to chant, to command enough Latin to recite the Mass, and to be able to name the Ten Commandments, the seven sacraments, and the seven capital sins.[4]

It was only in the thirteenth century, and in part in response to heresy, that the Roman church established clear guidelines for lay instruction and practice, defining what it meant to be a Christian. The Fourth Lateran Council, held in Rome in 1215, required the laity to confess, do penance, and receive Mass once a year at Easter, or be cut off from the church and denied burial in consecrated soil. Most medieval Europeans were taught only the simplest version of Christianity, at best. Whether they accepted it and what they actually believed are very much open questions. We cannot assume a normative orthodox Roman belief in the absence of evidence. Further, the nature of orthodoxy itself is a complex problem. Perhaps real orthodoxy existed only in the minds of a handful of theologians. Perhaps, as one historian suggests, orthodoxy is best understood as ecclesiastical vested interest.

It is crucial, then, to recognize the difference between beliefs that were not a part of orthodox Roman teaching and heresy, the label that some authorities imposed on certain beliefs and actions in certain circumstances. The legal definition of heresy was based on this difference. It separated variant belief from heresy by insisting that heresy had to be "pertinaciously defended." A person had first to be instructed that his or her beliefs were not orthodox and then still defend them in order to be considered a heretic. Otherwise, those beliefs were simply error. In practice, the church's pursuit of heresy was highly selective. The central questions, then, concern the relationship between variant beliefs, the social construction of heresy, and the persecution of heretics. First, why were some beliefs categorized as heresy? Then, what was the relationship between the definition of some beliefs as heresy and the persecution of specific groups of people?

In *The Formation of a Persecuting Society* (1987), Robert I. Moore gives a provocative answer to these questions. Moore critiques the view that persecution was a reaction to the growing threat of heresy, arguing that persecution arose in the twelfth century as a consequence of the rise of the state and the centralization of power. He points out that similar measures were taken to define and restrict a number of deviant groups in the twelfth and thirteenth centuries, including not only heretics but lepers and Jews. Like heretics, the Jews, already deprived of many legal rights, were required to wear identifying clothing and were banned from public office; lepers were cruelly segregated and literally deprived of legal existence. Similar stereotypes were ascribed to these three groups: heretics, Jews, and lepers were all linked with the devil and had voracious sexual appetites, a peculiar filthiness and stench, and so forth, ad nauseam. Each group posed a growing threat to Christendom. The attribution of the same stereotypical qualities to all these groups in the same period, Moore argues, was not accidental.

In Moore's view, then, persecution cannot be explained as reaction to the popularity of heresy, a Jewish conspiracy, and an epidemic of leprosy. The stereotypes were in fact the creation of a new, literate clerical elite that used the definition and exclusion of deviants as a means of reinforcing its claim to power. This elite group created and imposed the stereotypes and the institutional mechanisms for the persecution of those newly defined as deviant. In effect, Moore stands the problem of heresy on its head: heresy becomes the result of the need to persecute.

This is a compelling argument. However, it is not obvious that it accurately explains the conflict between the Roman and Cathar churches. Moore's model depicts a dominant orthodox tradition defining variant subgroups as deviant. The Waldensian heresy fits this view neatly, but does Catharism? Variant belief included, after all, not only deviations from Roman orthodoxy, but beliefs that, while based on Christian texts, were fundamentally different from Roman Christianity. The Waldensians, as Strayer explained, were initially a group of laypersons who sought to imitate the life lived by the apostles and to preach reform. They originally broke with the church not over the central elements of Christian theology but because they disobeyed the prohibition on lay preaching. Their condemnation as heretical was almost a historical accident. As Strayer suggested, Francis of Assisi became a saint while Peter Waldo, founder of the Waldensians, became a heretic in part because different popes made the decisions: the brilliant Innocent III was able to embrace rather than exclude Francis. The Waldensian movement was in essence an offshoot of Roman Christianity, originally similar to other reform movements—like the Franciscans—that were deemed orthodox.

Catharism was different. It did not begin as a critique of Roman practice and then become more radical with persecution; it was from the beginning a different religion, based on Scripture but irreconcilable with Roman Christianity. Thus, it is misleading to view the Cathar faith as variant belief constructed as heresy by the Roman church. Catharism was spread into Europe by a missionary effort. The conflict was a struggle between two competing religions.

Epilogue

Can one conclude that the Albigensian Crusades and the persecution of the Cathars was, from the perspective of medieval Rome, justified by the threat? That depends on one's evaluation of the success of the Cathars. How and when did the heresy spread? Did the Cathars succeed in organizing a widespread church? What social groups were drawn to the movement? What proportion of the population was involved? Most important, what did people actually believe? Can the population be divided into Cathar and Roman, or was actual belief more complex?

This epilogue will explore the problem of southern French heresy by looking at a series of contemporary texts. Heresies are inextricably tied to the texts that describe them. Some scholars would now argue that the recovery of actual thirteenth-century belief is impossible; we cannot get past the text and our modern preconceptions to reconstruct actual past beliefs with any accuracy.[5] This may well be true, but the effort to recover past belief on its own terms and to understand the process of the social construction of deviance is nevertheless a valuable one.

Variant beliefs are transmitted to us through texts, often written by hostile authors; the study of medieval heresy, therefore, consists of the close analysis of written documents. Indeed, in *The Implications of Literacy* (1983), Brian Stock has made the intriguing suggestion that medieval heresy was closely associated with textuality. He argues that the twelfth century saw a shift from an oral culture to a culture reliant on the written word. This shift changed both the structure of religious belief and the ways in which beliefs were communicated. Dissenting religious groups formed around texts and used them to structure their beliefs and actions. Critics of these movements turned to written texts in order to make sense of them. Whether or not one fully agrees with Stock, the essential point is that the study of medieval heresy is inseparable from the study of a series of complex texts. Texts not only provide us with evidence for heresy, but, used both by dissenters and by their critics, were actually constitutive of the heresies themselves.

This epilogue can by no stretch of the imagination be called a comprehensive survey of research on southern French heresy. Heresy—particularly Catharism in the south of France—has been one of the most intensively studied problems in medieval history, and there is a large and complex body of scholarship. The epilogue can only introduce a few of the questions addressed in that scholarship and explore some of the texts.

The Spread of Dualism

Significantly, popular heresy appeared at a definite moment: there is very little mention of it until the eleventh century, when suddenly a number of references appear in the chronicles. What this implies has been the subject of much debate. Again, the view that little variation from orthodoxy existed before the eleventh century would be hard to defend. There is evidence that other systems of belief were widespread: penitential manuals, guides written to aid priests in imposing penances for sin, listed many sins, such as magical practices, that imply non-Christian beliefs. These beliefs simply were not viewed as heresy by the authorities.

Historians of early medieval heresy were long preoccupied not with the relationship between non-Christian beliefs and heresy, but with the transmission of specific heretical ideas. Did heretical ideas spread, as many medieval authors suggested, as infection from earlier heresies? Or were they spontaneously generated, the product of medieval conditions? One specific question has been whether there was a direct link between medieval dualism and ancient Manicheanism, the dualist faith that for a period in the fourth century attracted Saint Augustine.[6] The eleventh-century sources often suggest a connection: when authors labeled particular beliefs as heresy they used ancient terminology, and even called deviants Manichees. Yet because these authors turned to texts from the Church Fathers, and in particular to Augustine's writings on the Manichees, for models to explain deviant belief, their writings can give the impression of a historical connection where none in fact existed. For example, Adhemar of Chabannes described as Manichees a group of people who appeared in Aquitaine around 1018 and who denied baptism and the Cross and "abstained from food and seemed like monks; they pretended chastity but among themselves practiced every debauchery."[7] In fact, if the accusations of debauchery are set aside, the group sounds like an evangelical movement. There is nothing in the description to suggest dualism other than the label *Manichee*. Most scholars would now agree that this does not mean that medieval heresies were direct descendants of ancient dualism.

Medieval dualism originated instead in Bulgaria in the tenth century. Its spread into the south of France was probably rather late, perhaps the mid–twelfth century. The Bulgarian origins of the faith are intriguing. The Bulgars were a tribe, rather like the Mongols, that conquered the Slavonic peoples. Bogomilism, as the Bulgarian faith was called, arose shortly after the conversion of Bulgaria to Christianity, during the long imposition of political and religious domination by the Byzantine Empire. In the tradition of the Eastern Church, political and religious authority were tightly interwoven, with church institutions under imperial control. A series of wars with the empire left Bulgaria, at the accession of Tsar Peter in 927, "with its economy in ruins, its army decimated in distant adventures, its aristocracy seething with humiliation, and its peasantry with discontent."[8] With Byzantine control came the heavy taxation of urban populations. The extension of large landed estates, many of them owned by the church, contributed to a new subordination of the peasantry. Many peasants lost their claim to their lands, sometimes ending up in servitude, sometimes as vagrants.[9]

Bogomil and his followers spoke directly to the peasants' economic and political concerns. The first clear account of the Bogomils is a detailed attack in a sermon written after 967 by Cosmas the Priest. The text reveals direct experience of the movement. Bogomil, according to Cosmas, combined a dualist cosmology with emphasis on apostolic simplicity and a direct challenge to public authority. The followers of Bogomil traveled and preached and practiced voluntary poverty. They denied all sacramental and ritual practices that were not demonstrably present in the New Testament, including infant baptism, the Mass, and confession to priests, as well as the cult of the saints and their relics. While they were pacifist, they did challenge secular and ecclesiastical authority. Cosmas in fact blamed the heresy partly on monastic corruption. One Bogomil text from the eleventh century also directly connects social and economic discontent and religious faith: it depicts Satan coaxing the angels in heaven to rebel against God by promising to cut their taxes![10] The Bogomil faith was spread within the Byzantine Empire by missionaries in the eleventh century, taking hold in Constantinople itself.

The first unquestionable evidence of Bogomil missionaries in western Europe is a letter written in 1143 by Eberwin, the prior of a religious house near Cologne, to enlist the aid of Saint Bernard of Clairvaux.[11] There were two heretical groups in the area. One group was new and especially threatening. Judging from the letter, these were converts to

Bogomilism: Eberwin described among other things the institutional divisions of the church into perfects and ordinary believers, the mode of life of the perfects, and the Cathar sacrament of the consolamentum. Another letter, this time from the clergy of Liège, dated 1145, tells a similar story. There is also evidence of the success of the heresy in the region around the Meuse, Rhine, and Moselle rivers between 1143 and 1167. After that time, dualism persisted in the region in competition with other faiths considered heretical. Its real success, however, was in the south.

Until the 1140s, accusations of heresy are more common in northern sources than in those of the south. There are only a few scattered examples of southern heresy, including Adhemar's "Manichees" in Aquitaine in 1018. Two celebrated preachers, Peter of Bruys and Henry of Lausanne, enjoyed some success in the south but did not begin there. Henry was a "black monk," a renegade from the Benedictine order, who enjoyed a long career as a popular preacher. He criticized the morals and authority of the priesthood and advocated lay moral reform through penance and austerity. Henry differed from orthodox reformers only in degree. Some texts mention popular disaffection from the church, and scholars have argued on this basis that Catharism was already present in Occitania in the 1140s, but as Robert Moore has argued, the sources do not make unquestionable references to Cathar faith or practice.[12]

Epilogue

In 1145 the great clergyman Bernard of Clairvaux traveled to Toulouse on a preaching mission against Henry of Lausanne. The accounts of his trip offer a window into popular religious disaffection in the decades before the spread of Catharism. Bernard wrote, in an often-quoted letter announcing his plans, of the dismal state of the southern churches: "The churches are without congregations, congregations are without priests, priests are without proper reverence, and finally, Christians are without Christ."[13] The Toulousans "laugh at prayers."[14] One of Bernard's companions, Geoffrey, the bishop of Chartres, wrote that many of the *textores* (weavers) were drawn to Henry's heresy, and were called *Arianos*—a term used to name an ancient group of heretics, the Arians.[15]

Geoffrey's mention of the *textores* became central to a long debate among historians over whether medieval heresy expressed socioeconomic grievances. Did the identification of weavers with heresy in this text and others mean that heresy had a special attraction for discontented urban workers, particularly those in the growing textile industries? The consensus now is that while the terms for weavers and heretics became linked, there is little evidence to suggest that textile workers—or artisans and workers more generally—were especially heretical. Historians have moved away from the idea that heresy was primarily a vehicle for the expression of social and economic discontent.[16]

Occitanian Social Structure

Geoffrey's letter also suggested that members of the knightly class were especially disaffected. His comment on the knights of Toulouse was revealing: "We found many of the knights to be obstinate, not so much from error as from greed and ill will, it seemed to us. They hate the clergy, and they enjoy Henry's witticisms, because the things he says give them an occasion and excuse for their evil."[17] There is considerable evidence to suggest that, unlike the weavers, knights actually were especially anticlerical and even heretical.

Who were these anticlerical knights? In order to understand their circumstances, we need to look back briefly at the development of the twelfth-century social structure in Occitania, and explore the relationship between the knights, the upper nobility, and public authority.[18] Strayer touched on these questions briefly and assumed long-term institutional continuity. He considered that Charlemagne's ninth-century empire put in place a set of governing institutions. After the empire collapsed, those institutions gave rise to feudal ties— a military nobility connected by networks of vassalage in which individual lords and vassals exchanged fief for homage and loyal service. In Occitania, the ties of vassalage became meaningless over time, a change Strayer attributed to the large number of nobles and the fragmentation of holdings.

Recent models of the formation of the nobility stress not

institutional continuity but rupture in the eleventh century. According to these models, feudal relations did not develop out of Carolingian institutions. Public authority persisted in the south of France into the eleventh century: the count of Toulouse adjudicated legal cases because he held a public office that ultimately derived from the Carolingian kings. After 1020, this public authority broke down. A period of radical instability followed, linked to growth in population and the economy. Small-scale wars between noble families became endemic; the sources are full of complaints of noble violence and disorder.

During the disorder of the eleventh century, a "militarization" of society took place. One element was castle building. Nobles reacted to disorder and the lack of stable public authority by building fortresses, both to protect their territories and to establish bases for assaults on their neighbors. One historian counted seventy-four castles built in the Languedoc between 975 and 1050, and this number is demonstrably far from comprehensive.[19]

These changes had a marked impact on the peasantry. Settlement patterns shifted as populations moved to live together and concentrated around castles or monasteries for protection. Many villages constructed walls for their defense. At the same time, because of the breakdown of public authority, local nobles were able to exercise powers of the state as territorial lords. Territorial lords could exercise over the peasants any of a number of specific rights. They required hospitality for themselves and their troops, exacted justice and a tax called the *taille*, levied labor, and controlled market rights and tolls.

The castles constructed in the period were occupied by armed *milites*, or knights. The knights were a new and populous social group at the bottom ranks of the nobility. The title identified a man as a professional warrior, trained to fight on horseback; many knights evolved from household warriors, the armed retainers of noble families. From the eleventh century, bands of knights appear in the sources, often acting as the military clients of more powerful nobles.[20] These nobles sought to control the knights by subordinating them to their private authority; whether the tie of vassalage was used is much debated. Some historians have argued that the feudal tie of vassalage as it existed in northern France was not used and in fact did not appear in the Languedoc until it was employed there by the northern French as a result of the Albigensian Crusades.[21] Others, including Pierre Bonnassie, argue that vassalage became pervasive in the twelfth century.

In the twelfth century, then, Languedoc included a handful of powerful noble families, the most important of these being the counts of Toulouse and Barcelona. Other noble houses were theoretically under their control but effectively independent: families like the Trencavel and the viscounts of Albi, of Béziers, of Carcassonne. The other great lords in the region were the bishops. Below this level there were numerous houses of lesser nobles, some independent, some clients of the upper nobles. And at the bottom of the nobility were the knights.

The most notable aspect of the structure of power in twelfth-century Languedoc was the absence of strong authority, public or private. Jurisdictions were uncertain. Higher nobles had enormous difficulty controlling their domains. It is startling evidence for the weakness of government that peace associations may have been the best working form of territorial political organization. The peace association was originally a clerical effort to place controls on noble violence by persuading nobles to take an oath restricting the practice of war. The second half of the twelfth century saw the rise of the "instituted peace," in which written definitions of peace were used as regulations governing noble behavior. The instituted peace even included provisions for armies to enforce the rules: participants took an oath not only to uphold the peace and perhaps serve in the enforcing army, but to pay a peace-tax to support the army and compensate victims. Peace associations filled some of the vacuum created by the absence of public administration.[22]

As Strayer pointed out, twelfth-century urban populations also joined together in associations bound by oaths. Towns had existed continuously from Roman times and in the twelfth century experienced rapid economic and demographic growth. Town populations characteristically held a mix of urban and rural backgrounds and interests. Knights from the castles and villages often moved into the towns and became engaged in urban ventures and urban politics while keeping their properties and other ties to the countryside. At the same time, the towns began to develop an urban nobility, patricians whose wealth came from banking or merchant ventures but who were titled knights and fought on horseback. The nobility within a town like Toulouse thus became a complex mix of families of various origins and interests.

In the late twelfth century, the wealthy and growing towns pressed for independence. For example, Toulouse was in theory under the rule of the count of Toulouse, but the town gradually usurped his powers. By 1200 the Toulousans effectively ruled themselves, by a system of consuls modeled on those of Italian towns. Efforts by the count to regain control were effective only briefly. Some rural communities established forms of collective association in imitation of the rising towns. From the late twelfth century evidence survives of the beginnings of village self-government: "prud'hommes," local big men, administered the village church and charitable institutions. This was in part a peasant initiative, in part an outgrowth of the lord's council. After 1200, self-governing consulates began to appear in some villages.[23]

The Early Spread of Catharism

Early accounts of Catharism in Occitania strongly suggest that it was attractive to the knights. Catharism may not have arrived in Occitania before the 1160s. There are a few problematic (and much debated!) texts. Heribert, a monk from Perigueux, wrote of false prophets whose voluntary poverty and denial of the validity of the sacraments had a special appeal for nobles and clerics. Heribert assumed that the devil was actively influencing the movement. Its converts could not be returned to Roman orthodoxy, he explained, because when they joined the group they automatically became literate: "Nobody is so stupid that if he joins them he will not become literate within eight days." They also had a diabolical ability to escape confinement: "Even if they are bound in iron chains and shackles, and put in a wine butt turned upside down on top of them, and watched by the strongest guards, they will not be found the next day unless they choose to be and the empty butt will be turned up again full of the wine which had been emptied from it."[24] Whether these diabolical agents were Cathar dualists is unclear.

In the summer of 1165, the bishop of Albi arranged a colloquy with a group of religious dissidents in Lombers, a walled village or *castrum* south of Albi. The village and castle were the property of the bishop and were held by a "consortium" of knights, all from the same lineage.[25] The extant account of the meeting is in some ways problematic, and it may be that several versions were awkwardly put together.[26] According to the text, the knights of Lombers supported the "good men," as the accused were called. Five "assessors" were "chosen and assigned by each of the two sides," a phrase that suggests not an inquisition but a more balanced debate. They were the bishop of Lodève, three abbots, and a man called Arnold Beben. The list of witnesses suggests the proceedings were thought important: four more bishops, one of them the archbishop of Narbonne; four more abbots; and a handful of priors, provosts, and archdeacons. This impressive clerical roster shows that the upper clergy feared the heresy, perhaps out of genuine pastoral concern for the people being led astray.[27] The laity at the assembly included three members of the upper nobility: Constance, the wife of Count Raymond of Toulouse, and two of her viscounts, Raymond Trencavel of Béziers and Sicard of Lautrec. Also present were "almost the whole population of Albi and Lombers, together with people of other towns."

The proceedings as reported in the sources were half inquiry and half debate. The bishop of Lodève questioned the good men about their beliefs, with an emphasis not on theology but on practice, on the sacraments. The good men avoided admitting to heresy but made their disaffection plain. They would accept only the authority of the New Testament. In what must have been a dramatic moment, given the audience of bishops and abbots, the good men launched a direct attack on the wealth of the clergy. If those who were ordained were not the sort of bishops and priests that Saint Paul called for in his epistle, then

> they were not bishops and priests but ravening wolves, hypocrites and seducers, lovers of salutations in the marketplace, and of the chief seats and the higher places at

table, desirous of being called rabbis and masters, contrary to the teaching of Christ, wearers of albs and gleaming raiment, displaying bejeweled gold rings on their fingers. . . . They were wicked, not good teachers but hired servants.[28]

After a debate in which each side hurled New Testament passages at the other, the bishop of Lodève condemned the sect as heretics. The good men responded with a denial of his authority: he was a ravening wolf and a hypocrite. The bishop offered to charge them formally with heresy in any Catholic court, including that of the pope, the French king, the count of Toulouse, Constance the count's wife, or the Trencavel viscounts. (This startling lack of clearly defined legal channels underscores the weakness of public authority.) The good men backed down, but in an odd way. Turning to the people watching the debates, they first carefully stated that they were doing this out of love for the people and then made a full orthodox profession of faith. However, they refused to swear to their professed faith, on two grounds. The first was a position actually rather common in the period, among orthodox believers as well as Cathars: oath taking was prohibited in the gospel. The second was the interesting assertion that the bishop of Albi had made a prior agreement with them that they would not have to take an oath. The bishop denied it. The assembly came to an end with the good men condemned for wrong views on oath taking.

What do these odd proceedings reveal? The faith of the good men was clearly popular. They were anticlerical, biblical fundamentalists. Indeed, their statements recall those of Henry of Lausanne. There is nothing in the text that conclusively shows them to have been dualists, although it is the first known appearance of the term *boni homines* (good men), which came to refer to Cathar holy persons or "perfects." Probably these men were Cathars, and their lack of clarity was a conscious strategy. They made their criticisms of the Roman church obvious to their audience but avoided a risky confession of heresy.

The upper clergy were improvising. The bishop of Albi was clearly unhappy that his knights supported these good men. Significantly, the meeting concluded with his warning to the knights to stop doing so. Evidently the bishop was afraid of losing authority over his knights and his walled village. He may have been enough of a politician to make an arrangement with the good men in advance, as they claimed. But again, the weakness of public authority is significant. It is clear that the bishop was unable to coerce; he must have thought that an open confrontation would be effective. But if he hoped not only to intimidate the knights and villagers but also to persuade them back to the fold, the plan certainly backfired: the spectacle of the simply dressed good men urging reliance on the gospel and attacking the richly garbed members of the upper clergy for their gold rings and hypocrisy can hardly have drawn the villagers or the knights back to the Roman church!

Cathar Organization and Spread

How successful were the Cathars in organizing an alternative church? There is startling evidence that the Cathar churches were well established by the 1170s. An extraordinary document, dated between 1174 and 1177, reveals a council of Cathar bishops meeting in order to establish diocesan boundaries. The text exists only in a late and much recopied version and presents many difficulties. On these grounds, Yves Dossat considered that it was forged by its seventeenth-century copyist. However, Bernard Hamilton has set many of these concerns to rest by arguing that it is an awkward combination of three earlier texts.[29] A Byzantine missionary called Papa (pope or perhaps father) Nicetas presided over the council and reconsecrated the western European bishops. There were six: a bishop of Lombardy, in northern Italy; a bishop of the French, which of course meant the northern French; and bishops of Albi, Toulouse, Carcassonne, and Agen in Occitania. Provisions were made to establish diocesan boundaries.

Papa Nicetas also preached a sermon, a fragment of which appears in the text. We have evidence concerning his mission from two Italian sources, which tell us that it was an effort to bring about unity in doctrine. The western European churches had been established by Bulgarian missionaries, who taught mitigated dualism. Nicetas, who came from Constantinople, sought to convert them to Byzantine absolute dualism. Mitigated dualists believed that the devil was subordinate to God and even God's creation; it was his rebellion from God's authority that brought about the disastrous creation of humankind. Absolute dualists believed in a cosmos divided between good and evil principles.[30] God created the world of spirit, the devil the world of matter.

The introduction of absolute dualism increased the tendency for Cathar churches to go into schism. The Occitanian churches are thought to have accepted the absolute dualism urged by Papa Nicetas; the Italians fragmented over the issue. The debate over this essential point of doctrine was one reason the Cathar churches did not enjoy institutional unity comparable to that of the Roman church; despite the fears of their opponents, they never posed the threat of a single, monolithic dualist church in western Europe.

The other institutional source of schism was the Cathar belief that the validity of a sacrament depended on the sanctity of the priest. This view had been argued by the Donatists in the Roman church at the time of Saint Augustine and ultimately condemned. Cathars believed that if a person received the consolation from an immoral perfect, then it was invalid, and any sacraments the person with the invalid consolation went on to administer would be invalid as well. There were several episodes in which a Cathar community learned to its horror that the original sacrament administered to the founders of its church was invalid because the perfect in question was immoral. The group would then need to find a perfect of unquestioned sanctity and start all over again. The author of "De heresi catharorum" recounts one example: after the Lombard community received a new consecration from Nicetas, a traveler told them that Nicetas's consecration was invalid because it ultimately derived from the bishop Simon, who had subsequently been found "in a room with a woman."[31] The ensuing debate over the possible need for reconsecration split the community. The general result—especially in the quarrelsome Italian towns—was a number of churches that did not recognize each other's sacraments. Despite the council of Saint-Félix, the Cathars never posed an organized, united institutional threat to the Church of Rome.

In 1176, Raymond V, count of Toulouse, complained to the pope that his city was overrun with heresy. In response, Alexander III sent a legation, supported by the French and English monarchs. Two letters describe the mission; one of them, written by Henry, abbot of Clairvaux, has been included as an appendix to this volume, "Heresy in Toulouse in 1178." The accounts of the mission give a particularly vivid and concrete glimpse of the Cathars in late twelfth-century Toulouse and of the efforts against them. The legate and his companions found the city full of heresy: Henry writes that when they first rode through town, heretics jeered and pointed at them, calling them apostates and heretics.

The legate summoned people suspected of heresy to make a profession of faith. Ironically, the legate had the two leading Cathars in Toulouse in his hands and did not know it. They were Bernard Raimundi, in fact the Cathar bishop of Toulouse, recently consecrated by Papa Nicetas, and Raymond de Baimac, who had played a major role at the Council of Saint-Félix as well. A letter of the legate himself, Cardinal Peter of St. Chrysogono, describes their questioning. Like the efforts of the clergy at Lombers in 1170, these proceedings were improvised. Bernard and Raymond—like the good men of Lombers—negotiated for a safe conduct before they appeared before the legate. There was a revealing debate over whether they should be allowed to discuss the faith in the vernacular. The two men initially produced a written account of their faith and then were questioned on it. They were asked to speak in Latin, "both because some of the legation did not understand their [Occitan] and because the Gospel and Epistles, which they wished to use to confirm their faith, were known to be written in eloquent Latin." One of them made the attempt but, the cardinal wrote, "could barely put two words together in Latin so that it became necessary for [the legation] to condescend because of their ignorance and to exchange words with them concerning the sacraments of the church in the vernacular, despite the absurdity."[32] This power struggle over language recalls

Epilogue

Stock's argument for the centrality of texts and language to heresy.

Like the good men of Lombers, Bernard and Raymond made a full profession of orthodox faith. They explicitly denied dualism and affirmed monotheism, transubstantiation, infant baptism, marriage, various religious orders, and even the obligation to pay tithes. Many witnesses, including the count himself, were outraged: they thought the profession was insincere and the two men were liars. Bernard and Raymond had formerly preached "that there were two gods, one good and one evil, and that the good god created those invisible things that cannot change or decay, while the evil god created the heavens, the earth, man and other visible things." They had denied that an unworthy priest could celebrate the Mass, that a man and wife could be saved if the marriage debt had been paid,[33] that an infant could benefit from baptism. When the two men refused to swear to their profession of orthodox faith, they were excommunicated and threatened with exile if they preached heresy.

This encounter with the Cathar leaders of Toulouse was not mentioned by Henry of Clairvaux. The real target of the investigation, according to Henry, was Peter Maurand. Peter was a man of wealth, status, and connections. Called a Cathar John the Evangelist, he was at the center of Toulousan heresy. Henry's account of Peter's questioning and recantation celebrates the triumph of orthodoxy. He told the story of Peter's initial intransigence, his dramatic breakdown and

201

confession when confronted with the relics of the saints, and his subjugation and humiliating penance. The account is odd, since a well informed, devout Cathar would only be repelled by relics, often bits of the corpses of the saints. The improvised quality of the proceedings is underscored by the text of Peter's recantation. The legate seems to have set aside the whole question of dualism and focused on Peter's admission of heresy concerning the Mass. He was made to recite words first written for an eleventh-century theologian who was forced to abjure his views on the real presence of Christ in the Eucharist. The choice of this abjuration suggests a special concern to stress Christ's physical nature and literal presence in the Mass.[34] Peter was also required to appear naked and barefoot every Sunday in the churches of Toulouse, to be scourged with rods; to surrender his rights to tithes (taxes owed to church institutions but in twelfth-century Languedoc often taken over by lesser nobles and knights); and to serve the poor in Jerusalem for three years.

Was Henry correct about Peter Maurand's high status? John Mundy's extensive reconstruction of the Maurand family certainly supports him. The Maurand in fact fit the view that knights were especially drawn to heresy. A lineage dating only from the mid–twelfth century, they were closely liked to the Toulousan monastery of Saint-Sernin and perhaps owed their initial wealth and status to control of church resources. Along with urban properties, they held substantial farms in the country, largely at nearby Valsegur, including the rights to tithes mentioned in Peter's condemnation.

The Maurand were an important family in Toulouse and, from 1141, served in the count's court and then as consuls. Were the orthodox authorities powerful enough to carry out the sentence against Peter? He was made to perform a dramatic and humiliating public penance, and in a settlement of 1179 the Maurand did surrender tithes to the monastery of Saint-Sernin. On the other hand, while Peter may have made his pilgrimage to Jerusalem, he was back in Toulouse in 1187, when he acquired properties from his kinsmen. He certainly was not ruined. A Peter Maurand served as consul five times between 1183 and 1215; if the Peter Maurand questioned in 1178 actually was a perfect, he would not have agreed to hold the office. The consul in that case was probably his son, also named Peter. Mundy concluded that the family was heavily Cathar. Nevertheless, they prospered in the thirteenth century.[35] The authorities were successful in imposing a penance, but it had little real impact.

How widespread was the heresy? Henry of Clairvaux's letter is ambivalent: he first evokes a city rife with heresy, then describes general relief at the orthodox triumph over Peter Maurand. How Cathar was Toulouse, and Occitania more generally? The most systematic clues for the real extent of heresy are in the records of the Inquisition. Unfortunately, these accounts are late, dating from after 1233. People did describe to the tribunal events in the distant past, so the records give some account of the heresy before the onset of persecution, but they are obviously flawed. The question these texts best address is the number of actual perfects—men and women who had received the sacrament and joined the Cathar equivalent of the priesthood. Witnesses were asked to name every perfect they had encountered and to describe what had taken place. A number of scholars have worked through those records, counted the number of perfects, and then estimated how many more went unmentioned. The best text is the huge inquest of 1245–46, intended to reach all males over fourteen and females over twelve. Five thousand six hundred and four witnesses were questioned, most of them from the Lauragais, the region between Carcassonne and Toulouse. These witnesses mentioned 719 perfects.[36] Jean Duvernoy counted 1,015 perfects named in testimony ending with this inquest and argued that the actual number of perfects was two or three times that figure. This seems high. Walter Wakefield, after evaluating these and similar estimates, made the reasonable guess that there were one thousand to fifteen hundred perfects in the Languedoc in 1200.[37] Not all of them were committed perfects for life: some perfects left the Cathars to return to orthodoxy, and a handful then changed their minds again and were reconsoled.[38]

The more important and difficult question is the ratio of perfects to believers. Not all perfects actively ministered to the laity. For example, Maurice Bécamel found in the Inquisition records of the diocese of Albi that no more than ten perfects were active at any given time. If converts are taken to be those who accepted Cathar teaching and received the deathbed sacrament, the consolamentum, the figures are startlingly small. Yves Dossat studied depositions to the inquisitors in 1245 from people of Le-Mas-Saintes-Puelles, a community that was considered a hotbed of heresy. In 420 depositions, only seven persons who had received the deathbed consolamentum in the past thirty-five years were mentioned.[39] Duvernoy pieced together the career of two Cathar bishops, Guilabert of Castres, active from 1193 to 1240, and Bertrand Marty, 1225–44. During those long periods, the sources reveal only forty persons who received the consolamentum.[40] It is worth noting that witnesses might have been reluctant to name those who received the consolamentum because of the dire consequences for their heirs. Nevertheless, these sources suggest that only a tiny portion of the population was full converts.

Evidence from the rich testimony collected by Jacques Fournier, bishop of Pamiers and later Pope Benedict XII, in the Fournier Inquisition, supports this conclusion, revealing people who were sympathetic to the Cathars but ultimately did not accept their sacrament. There are several dramatic cases of women who were drawn to Cathar teaching but refused the consolamentum for their ill children. Mengarde Buscalh testified that she had a sickly infant, two or three months old, and was urged to have him given the Cathar sacrament. Then, by allowing him to starve and die, she could ensure that he would remain pure and become an "angel of God." She refused, although she admitted that "it would have pleased her to have the child hereticated." Mengarde explained, "I said I'd never stop giving him my breasts as long as he was alive. For, as he was a Christian and had no sin except from me, I thought if I lost him God would take him."[41] Faced with this cruel choice, she took up a Roman understanding of original sin, baptism, and salvation.

How many people, like Mengarde, were sympathetic to the Cathars and believed some of their teachings but were not full converts? The number of people who might fall into this vague category was much larger. They were identified and pursued by the inquisitors, who penalized those who met with perfects, made them reverence, or aided them, and especially those who allowed the Cathar sacrament to take place in their homes. Actions are easier to demonstrate than belief. Undoubtedly, some people were penalized who were by no stretch of the imagination Cathar. In one pathetic case from 1268, from Italy rather than southern France, a woman voluntarily went to the inquisitors to confess that when her servant Dyambra was dying, she begged for a Cathar perfect so that she could receive the consolamentum. The mistress honored Dyambra's wishes and sent for a perfect. Dyambra was consoled and the perfect given some food and sent on his way. After they heard the story, the inquisitors had the mistress's house destroyed![42] The mistress thus would be counted among those convicted of Catharism despite the fact that she did not believe in the faith and only respected the wishes of a dying servant. Conviction by the Inquisition does not necessarily imply Cathar belief.

Nevertheless, Inquisition records are the best evidence that we have. Unfortunately, the records survive only in pieces, so that most do not offer a comprehensive look at all of the people convicted in a particular town or region. The best source for an overall portrait is the 1279 amnesty from Toulouse.

Urban Heresy: The Case of Toulouse

A royal amnesty of 1279 opens a rare window onto the diffusion of heresy in an urban community. In that year, almost exactly a century after the mission that questioned Peter Maurand, the French king came to a general settlement with the town of Toulouse. A part of that settlement was amnesty for all the people whose inheritances had been subject to confiscation because they had been condemned for heresy. The condemned themselves were long dead; the point of the amnesty was to free their descendants from the threat of confiscation. The list, naming 278 persons, survives and has been extensively studied by John Mundy.[43] The amnesty is probably the most complete account we have of the real diffusion of heresy in a thirteenth-century town. Its compilers considered it a complete list of those guilty of heresy, and Mundy argues persuasively that it does not include those convicted of other crimes. The amnesty begins with the people who had penances imposed upon them by the papal legate Cardinal Roman in 1229, right at the end of the crusades, and extends through the successive efforts of the Inquisition, from 1233 up to those condemned in the 1270s. No one listed was condemned for actions after 1259. The amnesty thus offers the best evidence of the real extent of Catharism in one town over time.

What proportion of the population appears on the list? There are 278 names, 73 of them female. Mundy points out that only people with landed property subject to confiscation were listed. This means that women are underrepresented. Further, the list does not include those who received mild sentences and were not subject to confiscation. Mundy estimates these at 30 percent of the total number of convictions. If a proportionate number of women and people with milder sentences are added, he considers, the number climbs to 506 people. The total population was under twenty-five thousand.[44] Five hundred six, a mere two percent, seems a small number! Mundy considers the list "the tip of the iceberg": most of those who at least dabbled with divergent belief were not condemned for it.

Who was named? The most striking aspect of the list is the high proportion of elites. Twenty percent of the males belonged to families of urban nobles. Mundy argues there were five very conspicuous knightly houses in the city; members of four of them appear on the list. Less conspicuous but wealthy consular families, whose members also included titled knights, were heavily represented as well. Another 15 percent of the males came from recent "middle range" families: merchants, money changers, notaries. Many of the consuls, the city's executives, appear. Below this level, roughly 25 percent of the men amnestied had craft or trade names. In sum, judging from this list, a high proportion of Cathar heretics came from the Toulousan elite.

However, to draw this conclusion would be to ignore the many drawbacks of the list as a social portrait of the heresy, drawbacks that underscore the complexity of the problem of reconstructing heresy and deviant belief. There is probably some elite bias: the inquisitors were going after the big fish whose conviction for heresy would make an impression, and whose property was worth confiscating. Further, the fact that the Inquisition convicted these people does not mean that all were committed Cathar believers. One man was burned for heresy—at least according to his wife—because of sympathy for a living creature: "He was unwilling to kill a chicken at the order of the Inquisitors, but said that the chicken had done nothing wrong and did not deserve to die."[45] Perhaps the man was a Cathar, but perhaps not.

Probably only a small fraction of the population of Toulouse was fully committed to Catharism. These were the true converts, people who were convinced of the truth of the Cathar faith and the falsity of Roman Christianity. Again, the best measure of their conviction is their willingness to reject the sacraments of the Roman church in favor of the Cathar consolamentum. If they were wrong, they were guaranteeing their own damnation. A larger proportion of the population was sympathetic to Catharism, but not fully converted. They heard Cathar preaching, respected and in some cases even aided the perfects. This does not mean that they were committed Cathars. The faith was imbedded in the community, tolerated and in fact admired by non-Cathars. One man was asked by the bishop of Toulouse to explain why he took no action against known Cathars. He answered, "We cannot expel the heretics: we were raised with them, have kin among them and we see them live honestly."[46] This individual was convinced that it was the bishop who preached the true faith, but many of his neighbors were less certain.

Why were people attracted by Catharism? This question has been endlessly debated and certainly will not be resolved here. The heresy was clearly fostered by the lack of strong public authority characteristic of Occitania in the twelfth century; yet this does not explain Catharism's core attraction. As we have seen, historians have become dissatisfied with the view that heresy was primarily an expression of socioeconomic discontent. It is important to understand the Cathars against the background of the larger spiritual currents of the twelfth and thirteenth centuries. Their motives were not unlike those of the Franciscans or the Waldensians. They shared the desire for a return to the poverty and simplicity of the apostles, and for personal spiritual renewal.[47] What set the Cathars apart was their complete break with the Roman church and their dualist understanding of sin and evil. In 1978, Malcolm Lambert offered an intriguing "characteristic psychology" of perfects, derived from analysis of their religious practices, their diet, their celibacy, the stories they preached. They understood evil not as a moral failure so much as pollution, a soiling; lapses in their strict vegetarian diet were the moral equivalent of a serious crime. A perfect was apt to be "a tense, rather literal-minded perfectionist with a strong determination, imaginative rather than logical power, perhaps with a tendency to organic disgust, anti-intellectual and not strongly religiously educated."[48] One could say much the same thing of Saint Francis! Perhaps the major difference is that Francis conquered his "organic disgust."

One common argument for Catharism's attraction is that it was an easy religion in practice.[49] While the perfects led very rigorous lives, ordinary believers were allowed great freedom. The Cathar church had no social teachings, as Ladurie has pointed out. Thus the Cathar faith was less demanding than Roman Christianity. One had only to receive the deathbed sacrament to be saved. This view ignores the considerable inconvenience and hardship suffered by Cathar believers in the period of persecution: it was not in this sense an easy religion. But perhaps people were attracted to a church that did not meddle with their everyday lives.

Two further approaches seek to relate Catharism to social and political structures while avoiding the straightforward socioeconomic argument that heresy expressed material grievances. These approaches attempt to understand the content of Cathar beliefs as responses to the social and political order. The first is the view that heresy was closely linked to anticlericalism. The second approach is to look at inheritance and family structure. Was the success of Catharism linked to elite patterns of inheritance and property ownership? In particular, did the heresy have a special attraction for women?

Anticlericalism, Clerical Corruption, and Papal Monarchy

As we have seen, the early texts describing heresy in Occitania reveal intense anticlericalism, but it is not always clear that they also reveal heresy. What was the relationship between the two? On the one hand, as Jacques Chiffoleau has pointed out, there has been a tendency among both medieval and modern authors to equate them: anticlerical texts imply the presence of heresy.[50] In Avignon, the town studied by Chiffoleau, popular movements arose in the 1230s and 1240s in which bishops were driven from their sees, tithes confiscated, lower clergy harassed, church property destroyed. Contemporary authors thought that this smacked of heresy: one archbishop explicitly wrote, "There is no doubt that such attacks, since they go against the praiseworthy custom of the church, should be suspected of heretical wickedness."[51] On the other hand, as Chiffoleau also points

out, the fact that people refused to pay tithes does not mean
that they were convinced by Cathar or Waldensian teaching;
it means only that they resented the economic and political
power of the clergy.

What caused anticlericalism, and was it appreciably
stronger in the regions where Catharism took hold than in
other parts of Europe? Many scholars have argued that
people were anticlerical because they considered the clergy
to be corrupt or hypocritical. This has led to debate over
whether the clergy were in fact more corrupt in the regions
where Catharism prospered. Some have argued, for example,
that heresy did not succeed in Provence because church
reform had already been successful there in the eleventh
century. The clergy there were of a higher caliber than those
in the Languedoc.

Were Occitanian clerics especially corrupt? Strayer's discussion is convincing. The local clergy were often ill-trained
and even corrupt, but no worse in Occitania than elsewhere.
The upper clergy may have been a different story. Secular
clerics are depicted by some contemporaries—ranging from
Innocent III to the good men of Lombers—as luxury-loving
hypocrites, hungry for power and wealth, and rarely present
in their dioceses. Regular clergy were also attacked. This was
clearly linked to anger over tithes. One piece of evidence is
quite late but does describe shocking corruption. In 1254 an
inquisition was held against the abbot of the monastery of
Lezat, near Toulouse. He was ultimately condemned for

simony, dilapidation of the monastery's wealth, breaches of order, and sexual incontinence. In the man's twelve-year career as abbot, he may have had sexual relations with thirty-five women, one of them a long-term concubine.[52] Accusations of clerical hypocrisy and corruption were at times justified.

Others argue that anticlericalism was not a reaction to clerical corruption but a struggle over power. People resented the growing power and wealth of the papacy and some elements of the clergy. Heresy was closely linked to competition between the nobility and the churches for wealth. Nobles who profited from usurped church resources were attracted to the preaching of Cathar perfects who told them that those resources actually should not belong to the church. Many anecdotes illustrate noble domination of particular churches. The Trencavel viscounts notoriously bullied clerics and treated churches as family property. When the monks of Saint Mary at Alet elected a new abbot without consulting the Trencavel's representative, he "invaded the monastery, imprisoned the abbot-elect, and, propping the exhumed corpse of the predecessor in the chair, had it preside over another election by the cowed remnant of monks."[53] The disputed resources were often rights to tithes; as we saw, Peter Maurand's penance for heresy included the obligation to restore the tithes his family had taken from Saint-Sernin.

For Jacques Chiffoleau, the central problem is not noble usurpations but the changing nature of clerical power. The thirteenth century saw a "pastoral revolution": a concerted effort to improve the spiritual care given to the laity and to reinforce the power and status of the clergy. This combined with a profound change in the economic base of church institutions. Churches suffered a period of economic crisis when their rents from agricultural lands dwindled; they responded by shifting to reliance on other sources of wealth, including testamentary bequests, payments for sacraments, and funding for prayers for the dead. Chiffoleau also argues that accusations of heresy were integral to the change: clerics constantly evoked the threat of heresy to justify their growing power and authority. At least in Provence, he argues, this does not mean that heretics were an actual threat.

The new economic bases of the churches were linked with the rise of the papal monarchy and changes in religious teaching, in particular the elaboration of medieval cosmology into the complex system elegantly articulated in Dante's *Divine Comedy*. The afterlife was divided into purgatory, heaven, and hell, ordered according to an elaborate hierarchy based on degrees of sin and of perfection. Only a handful of pure souls at death passed to heaven; the remainder either were condemned or had to undergo a period of purgation. The French historian Jacques LeGoff has argued that the idea of a special intermediate place of purgation was developed only in the high Middle Ages. Contact between the realm of the living and the realm of the dead was possible and in fact essential: the living could affect the fate of the dead by obtaining intercession to hasten their journey to paradise. That intercession was achieved through charity and prayer. The thirteenth century saw the rise of commemorative masses in which the living used funds to acquire prayers for the dead; this was also the period of the rise of death confraternities, in which lay people acquired merit through charity, then expended it in prayers for the dead.

Chiffoleau's approach is intriguing because it connects beliefs about death and salvation to anticlericalism. The argument in its most bald form would be that anticlericalism was a reaction against the elaboration of this view of the afterlife. It was a cosmology that reinforced clerical authority and encouraged lay donation to the church in hopes of intercession for souls in purgatory. In essence, it generated new sources of authority and revenue for the clergy. There is evidence to support this explanation of anticlericalism: Cathars who rejected clerical authority and the new model of the afterlife in the same breath. As we shall see, some individuals repudiated this complex, hierarchical afterlife and denied any need for intercession. People directly stated that prayers did not benefit the dead, or described alternative cosmologies in which everyone was saved, or depicted paradise as egalitarian. In effect, some people became anticlerical because they considered the local clergy corrupt hypocrites. But perhaps others resented the local clergy for doing their work well: teaching the need for intercession for the dead and gaining power and authority in consequence.

Epilogue

Anticlericalism was encouraged by the repression of heresy. The intense bitterness created by the crusades alienated people from the Roman church and drove some to Catharism. Saint Dominic and his followers, preaching in the Languedoc and living austere lives like those of the perfects, had converted a number of Cathars to Roman orthodoxy. During the crusades, some of these converts angrily returned to the Cathars. The plight of Bishop Fulk of Toulouse encapsulates both the financial problems of the church and lay anger over the crusades. The finances of the Toulousan bishopric were a disaster, largely because most tithes were diverted to knights and monasteries. When the reforming Bishop Fulk took office in 1205, he found that much of the episcopal property that remained was pledged to creditors who were pressing for repayment. He was actually forced to keep his mules hidden and have water carried to them in concealment. If the mules had been walked to the public fountain they would have been seized for debt![54] Bishop Fulk was a talented reformer who launched a confraternity as a combined attack on heresy and usury that initially enjoyed popular support in Toulouse. However, this success was squandered during the crusades. As Mundy writes, Fulk became "an exile from much of his diocese, wandering about with armies and given to bitter stories and angry rejoinders." In 1227 he was with the crusading army at the siege of a small town when the defenders called him not their bishop but the "bishop of devils." "Right they are," he answered, "they are devils and I am their bishop."[55] Ironically, the reforming Bishop Fulk himself was a victim of the crusades.

Women, the Family, and the Attractions of Heresy

Heresy was linked not only to attitudes toward the clergy but to life within the family. Crucial changes in inheritance customs that took place in the eleventh and twelfth centuries dramatically altered the situations of women. During this period, noble families consolidated to form patrilineages. The patrilineage redefined the family to emphasize male ancestry: a lineage considered itself a group of men descended from a shared ancestor, with that descent traced in the male line. There was a new, dynastic sense of the lineage as permanent, outlasting the lifetime of any individual. Surnames came into use as families identified themselves as lineages, for example, the Trencavel or the Castronovo.[56] New urban families like the Maurand adopted the same customs.

The formation of lineages was in essence a response to economic and demographic growth. Families wished to protect their properties from fragmentation: they feared that their resources could quickly be dissipated. When they acted as lineages, they shifted marriage and inheritance customs in order to hold their resources intact as patrimonies. Before this change, a portion of a man's estate had gone at his death to his wife, and the remainder probably was divided among his male and female children. This meant that substantial property might pass into the female line. In the new patrilineal custom, women were cut off from inheritance from either their fathers or their husbands. They received instead a Roman dowry as a marriage settlement. This sum, settled on a woman by her father, usually at her marriage, passed into the keeping of her husband. The purpose of the dowry was to guarantee a woman's status. A woman retained a permanent legal claim to her dowry: if her husband died she would recover the dowry and could remarry or live honorably as a widow. The exclusion of dowered women from inheritance meant that a share of the patrimony did not pass out of the lineage through marriage.

What of the property passed to sons? In Occitania, families tended to avoid fragmentation of the patrimony by transmitting it to their sons in undivided shares. A man with three brothers might receive a quarter share of his father's landed properties. His share was kept undivided, and in theory he and his brothers administered the property together and might even pass on their undivided shares to their heirs. The knights of Lombers are probably an example: a "consortium" of men from the same lineage, they apparently shared their rights to the walled village.

These customs, while promoting lineage solidarity, sacrificed the interests of the individual. It may be that some young men were left disaffected by their lack of economic independence and found an expression for their alienation in

Catharism. The case is stronger for women. After all, family solidarity was achieved at the direct expense of wives and daughters.

Many historians have suggested that the Cathar faith had a special attraction for women, particularly women from the elite. The heresy in fact was part of a larger movement of women into religious life in the twelfth and thirteenth centuries.[57] Some have argued that women were drawn to the heresy because of their social and economic circumstances; their heresy expressed their reaction to exploitation and oppression. It may also be that alienation from marriage, childbirth, and family drew some women to Catharism. Cathar dualism included a radical denial of any value to marriage, sexuality, and childbirth. As one witness in 1247 stated, the Cathars explicitly taught that matrimony was prostitution. And for a convinced Cathar, the conception of a child was a disaster: another spirit had been trapped in flesh. A woman called Aimersenda told the inquisitors that female perfects jeered at her when she was pregnant, claiming she carried a demon in her belly.[58] Aimersenda was angered and rejected Catharism, but other women reacted positively.

Other scholars have argued that women joined the Cathar church because it offered them the opportunity to become female priests, or perfectae, and administer the sacraments, a privilege denied them in the Roman church. This question was thoroughly researched by Richard Abels and Ellen Harrison, using as their main source the great inquest of 1245–46 in the Lauragais.[59] Again, 5,604 witnesses were questioned, and they named 719 Cathar perfects. Forty-five percent of the perfects were women. However, female perfects were less visible. The witnesses mentioned sighting some perfects repeatedly, implying that those perfects were particularly active. Women were mentioned less frequently than men: only 23 percent of the sightings of perfects were of females. Thus while women comprised almost half of the perfects, they were much less visible than men. Further, Abels and Harrison found that women almost never performed the sacrament and only rarely preached or debated publicly. Only eleven of the 318 female perfects mentioned by witnesses are known to have preached.

Before the onset of persecution, some of these women lived secluded in large hospices resembling orthodox convents, and many remained in small homes, sometimes with family. Their observances were similar to those of nuns in an orthodox convent: prayers and fasting. After the onset of persecution in the mid-1230s, this pattern changed as settled communities were broken up and many perfectae lived on the roads and in temporary hiding. At the same time, their numbers dropped, although those women who remained took on more active roles in preaching and performing the sacrament. All in all, Abels and Harrison concluded that the Cathar churches did not in practice offer women more active and powerful roles. Instead, the experiences of Cathar women roughly paralleled those of women in the Roman church.

Abels and Harrison also concluded that women were not

especially drawn to the heresy but joined the Cathars because their families were already involved. This is less convincing. The fact that a whole family accepted the heresy does not mean that women necessarily followed the conversions of their fathers, husbands, or brothers. How often did women convert first and then persuade the men of the household?[60] There are also cases of women who refused to accept Catharism despite the wishes of their families. Hylarda, the wife of William de Vilela, testified that she accepted the heresy at the urging of her husband and his father, but only for two days. Then a perfect angered her when he told her to take the candle she was making for the feast of the Virgin at the local church and burn it at home instead. After that, Hylarda testified, she was unwilling to believe the heretics.[61] Her initial conversion to Catharism cannot have been profound!

If one looks closely at the actual involvement of families, the most striking thing is that families tended to be mixed. Some members became Cathar, others did not. Mundy's extensive family reconstructions from the royal amnesty of 1279 best show this. To choose just one example, the chronicler Puylaurens mentions that a distinguished man of the Castronovo lineage called Aimeric Probushomo was condemned for heresy, as were his wife Constantia, one of his sons, Castellusnovus, and his son's wife Esclarmunda. Despite the condemnations, the Castronovo were able to preserve family property. Aimeric's nephews, two Castronovo brothers, served as leaders of Bishop Fulk's antiheretical confraternity, around 1206. One of them, Copha, changed sides during the crusades and dabbled in Catharism.[62] Of course, some households and families tended to be more sympathetic to Catharism; some welcomed and aided the perfects, and others did not. It is also the case that some people betrayed their kinfolk to the Inquisition.

Individual Belief

In the late twelfth and thirteenth centuries, some authorities—for the political and institutional reasons elegantly spelled out by Strayer—divided the population into orthodox believers and deviants. This division did reflect the success of the Cathar churches: probably as many as several thousand people accepted Cathar teaching to the point of placing their hopes of salvation in the Cathar sacrament and becoming perfects. To this extent, heresy posed a real threat. But what of the rest of the population? The texts that survive make it clear that the simple categories of Cathar and orthodox often are inadequate. How did contemporaries judge a person's orthodoxy?

The Dominican chronicler William Pelhisson recounts the story of a man called John Textor who, when questioned by the Inquisition, yelled to his fellow townspeople, "Gentlemen, listen to me!"

I am not a heretic, for I have a wife and I sleep with her. I have sons, I eat meat, and I lie and swear, and I am a faithful Christian. So don't let them say these things about me, for I truly believe in God. They can accuse you as well as me. Look out for yourselves, for these wicked men want to ruin the town and honest men and take the town away from its lord.[63]

This plea points up the reliance on practice to distinguish heretic from orthodox. John Textor insisted that he was not a heretic by citing how he ate, drank, slept, and spoke. People were condemned not for cosmological beliefs but for actions: they fed the perfects, heard them preach, received their sacrament.

Actual belief is more difficult to determine. John Textor's case is a good example. He was considered by the chronicler to be a hypocrite and a Cathar, but the story is ambiguous. After John was returned to prison, Pelhisson wrote, he "pretended to be sick" and begged for the Christian sacrament but was not given it. Then, when Cathar perfects were imprisoned with him, he accepted their sacrament. It was only after this encounter that he firmly professed the Cathar faith to the inquisitors and was burned for it. Perhaps he had justifiably feared death and simply wanted someone's sacrament! His conversion could actually have taken place in prison, a reaction to his treatment by the Dominicans.

How much can be known of actual belief? There are a few extant Cathar treatises, which set out versions of dualist theology in narrative form.[64] There are also descriptions written by inquisitors, in one case a former Cathar. The occasional first-person narratives reveal more of what people really knew of Catharism and of the beliefs they accepted. Not surprisingly, these texts suggest great variety of belief among the people considered Cathars.

One of the most detailed texts dates from 1247, when the committed Cathar Peter Garcias of Toulouse spoke several times with a kinsman, William, who belonged to the Franciscan order. The two men met in the common room of the Franciscan convent to debate Peter's Cathar beliefs. The discussions were a trap: with William's connivance, several other friars were hidden nearby to eavesdrop as Peter Garcias spoke freely of his faith. Six months later, the friars repeated Peter Garcias's statements to the Inquisition.

In part, Friar William and his heretical kinsman debated Cathar interpretation of Scripture. One of the hidden friars reported:

When Peter was asked by Friar William Garcias if he who was hung on the cross made these visible things, Peter answered, "No"; for He was the best, and nothing of these visible things is good. Therefore, He made none of them. . . . When Friar William Garcias spoke with Peter Garcias about the text, "In Him were all things created in heaven and on earth, visible and invisible," Peter said that it should be expounded; "Visible to the heart and

invisible to the eyes of the flesh." . . . Also, he heard
Peter Garcias saying that all the angels who fell from
heaven, and they alone, will be saved. . . . Christ and the
Blessed Virgin and the Blessed John the Evangelist came
down from heaven and were not of this flesh. . . . John
the Baptist was one of the greatest devils that ever was.
Also, he heard Peter Garcias, when Friar William Garcias
showed him his hand and asked if the flesh will rise
again, saying that the flesh will not rise again except as a
wooden post, striking a post with his hand.

Another hidden friar testified that

Peter said all who chanted in church, singing in unintelligible fashion, deceived simple people; and that in his
house he had a Passion, written in Romance, as it actually occurred. Peter also said that marriage performed by
the Roman Church, that is, of man and woman, for example, of him and his wife, Ayma, is prostitution; there is
no matrimony except that of the soul with God. And he
called the Roman church a harlot who gives poison and
the power to poison to all who believe in it. . . . Peter
also said that he had not in the carnal sense slept with
his wife since pentecost, two years ago. And when Friar
William remarked to Peter that this was because she was
of the same faith as his, he said no, but she was [a stupid
brute],[65] just as Friar William was. Peter also said of

miracles that no miracle which can be seen by the eyes is anything and neither the Blessed Francis nor any other person performed a miracle and that God desired no justice which would condemn anyone to death. . . . Peter said also that if he could lay hold of that God who would save only one out of a thousand men made by Him and would damn the others, he would break Him in pieces and rend him with nails and teeth as perfidious . . . only the angels who fell are to be saved, but not all such as the leaders and their assistants, only the ordinary ones, in such wise that not one of a thousand will be damned. Also Peter said there was no Purgatory and that alms given by the living are of no avail to the dead and no one is saved unless he does perfect penance before death and that a spirit which cannot do penance in one body, if it is to be saved, passes into another body to complete penance.[66]

Peter was a well-informed Cathar, literate in the vernacular and able to debate interpretation of Scripture. He was fully convinced of dualism and saw the implications of its denial of the physical. He was very quick to condemn the practices of the Roman church, its sacraments, unintelligible chanting, alms for the dead, cult of miracles. Perhaps the most striking thing about the account is his anger at the view that only a small minority of people will ultimately merit salvation: he was ready to attack with nails and teeth the God who would first create and then condemn the majority of humankind.

Some of these views are echoed in other testimony. Here is the cosmological myth told by the Cathar Pierre Authie, as recollected for the Inquisition by Sybille Peire, sixteen years later.

The heavenly father in the beginning made all spirits and souls in heaven, and they remained with him there. Then the devil went to the gate of paradise, wanting to enter, and could not. He remained at that gate for a thousand years. After that he entered paradise by a fraud, and, once inside, persuaded spirits and souls made by the heavenly father that all was not well with them, since they were subject to that father, but if they wanted to follow him and come to his world, he would give them possessions—fields, vineyards, gold and silver, wives, and other good things of this visible world.

At his persuasion, the misguided spirits and souls in heaven followed the devil, and all who accepted that persuasive course fell from heaven. So many fell, nine days and nine nights—they fell like the small rain. Then the heavenly father, seeing himself almost deserted by spirits and souls, arose from his throne and put his foot over the hole through which they were falling, and said of those who remained that if they moved to any extent from then onwards, they would never have peace or rest.

And to those falling he said, "Go for a time, for now." If he had said "from now on", not one of them would be saved or would return to heaven. But because he said "for now", that is, for some time, all those spirits will return to heaven—will return there with great difficulty and belatedly; but the spirits of simple folk, because they consented to leave heaven on impulse and as it were deceived by others, will return there swiftly and with ease.

After the world's end all this visible earth will be full of fire, sulphur and pitch, and will be burnt up—and this is what is called hell. But all human souls will then be in paradise, and in heaven one soul will have as great a good as the next, and all will be one, and the soul will love any soul whatever as much as the soul of its own father or mother or children.

Pierre spoke of fundamental cosmology: creation, punishment, and salvation. Yet it is a very tangible account: God literally got off his throne and put his foot on the hole in the floor to stop the continued fall of the angels from heaven! The angels—like some of Sybille's neighbors—were greedy for vineyards and wives, and unwilling to submit to authority. There is also a populist cast to the account. The simple folk who were deceived will return to heaven with ease; the rich and greedy will have to suffer first. There will be no inequities in rewards in heaven. This egalitarian paradise is very different from the ranked hierarchies of the Paradiso in Dante's *Divine Comedy*, written at roughly the same time. And Pierre's story as retold by Sybille was a very comforting one: in the end, the fires of hell will touch no one. All will be united and all will be saved.

This text comes from the extraordinary register of the Fournier Inquisition, which took place between 1318 and 1325, a full century after the crusades. While the evidence in the register is late, it is unparalleled because entire depositions were preserved. Most Inquisition registers contain only brief, boiled down versions, not statements of belief but bare narratives recounting who met and aided the perfects or received the Cathar sacrament. The Fournier register includes the entire narrative. It was used in the 1970s by the French historian Emmanuel Le Roy Ladurie to create a collective portrait of peasant social organization and beliefs in one village, Montaillou. Ladurie showed among other things the existence of magical and ghost beliefs alongside what was often a mix of Roman Christianity and Catharism.[67]

The register also allows us to hear individual voices and reminds us of the variety of individual belief and speculation. Some people were skeptics, like Guillemet Benet, who testified, "I can't see anything come out of men or women when they die. For if I saw their soul, or anything at all, coming out, I'd know that the soul existed. But as I see nothing, I can't make out what it is, the soul. . . . When men die, one only sees them expire, and their last breath is nothing but wind." Guillemet was not a Cathar but a materialist, unwilling to give credence to the notion of an immaterial soul, a soul that could not be touched or seen.

Other testimony reveals individuals blending Cathar teachings with Roman faith and their own conceptions. The most extraordinary was that of Grazida Lizier, a young peasant woman who carried on a long love affair with the notorious and very heterodox parish priest, Pierre Clergue. The affair took place with the encouragement of her mother, before and after Grazida's marriage. She broke it off only when she learned their relations were technically incestuous. Until that time, Grazida believed the affair was not a sin because of their mutual joy. She described her beliefs:

> I believe there is a paradise, for it is something good, as I've heard tell; I don't believe in hell (though I don't argue against it), for that is something evil, as people say. I've often heard that we shall rise again after death—I don't believe that, though I don't discredit it.
>
> I still believe it is no sin when love-making brings joy to both partners. I have believed that ever since Pierre first knew me. No one taught me these things except myself. I haven't taught them to others—no one has ever asked me about them.
>
> I believe God made those things that are helpful to man, and useful too for the created world—such as human beings, the animals men eat or are carried about

on—for instance oxen, sheep, goats, horses, mules—and the edible fruits of the earth and of trees. But I don't think God made wolves, flies, mosquitoes, and such things as are harmful to man; nor do I think he made the devil, for that is something evil, and God made nothing evil.[68]

Grazida denied the Cathars' radical condemnation of the physical world as fundamentally evil, the creation of the devil. Her concern was to absolve God of responsibility for evil and to affirm the goodness of those things that are useful or give pleasure, oxen and goats, grains and fruits. Her belief that lovemaking that gives mutual joy is not evil—a highly un-Cathar idea—evokes the whole troubadour celebration of love. Grazida, like Pierre Authie, denied the existence of a hell of eternal torment for sinners, but believed in paradise. She also recalls Guillemet's materialism: she could not believe in the resurrection of the dead.

In other testimony, ghost beliefs combined with variants of Christian teaching. Arnaud de Monesple, a medium in contact with the dead, consoled a woman who had recently lost a daughter. She reported that

he said the dead do no other penance than to walk at night from church to church, keeping vigil. And when I said, they must surely suffer when it's cold, he said the dead seek a house or place where there's a lot of wood

and warm themselves at a fire, and make the fire themselves. He told me that my daughter Fabrisse had come
to me and found me in my bed. . . . When he claimed
that she walked well, and as merrily as the other women,
I said, "And how could my daughter walk as quickly as
the others, since she died heavily pregnant?" And he
answered, "Your daughter is beautiful and strong . . . at
the coming feast of All Saints she will go to rest. No soul
of a grown man or woman enters paradise itself before
Judgement Day, only the souls of children who die before they are seven go at once into God's glory. . . .
Later, at the Judgement, all will be saved, so that no soul
of man or woman will perish or be condemned." I answered: "Please God that no one be condemned."

The testimony gives a moving picture of a woman finding consolation. The dead walk at night but do not suffer;
they make fires to keep themselves warm. Her daughter, who
had died in pregnancy, is beautiful and strong. Innocents,
children who die young, immediately enter paradise. And
ultimately, everyone will be saved.

This testimony comes from peasants in a remote village
in the Pyrenees; it cannot be assumed to represent the
beliefs of most Occitanians. Perhaps city dwellers—particularly people such as Peter Garcias, who owned a vernacular
Passion and could read it—were more apt to know and accept
an established faith. Still, these accounts forcibly remind us

of the narrowness of analyzing belief in terms of heresy and orthodoxy. Judging from these accounts, people wove together their beliefs, drawing on the teachings and practices of the Roman clergy, the Cathar perfects, their families, and their communities, as well as their own speculation and experience. Their beliefs are often similar: they shared with each other and with the Cathars certain preoccupations, including the source of evil, the status of the physical world, the limits of punishment. To call beliefs like those of Grazida Lizier heretical poses rather than answers a question.

NOTES

1. See the discussion in Gordon Leff, *Heresy in the Later Middle Ages* (New York, 1967), 1:1–3.

2. This was the definition of the thirteenth-century theologian Robert Grosseteste, quoted by Edward Peters in *Heresy and Authority in Medieval Europe* (Philadelphia, 1980), 4.

3. An influential proponent of the idea of a gap between elite and popular religious culture has been the French historian Jacques LeGoff; see, for example, his book *Time, Work and Culture in the Middle Ages* (Chicago, 1980). For a general survey of views of medieval Christianity, and the argument that the Middle Ages were essentially Christian, see John Van Engen, "The Christian Middle Ages as an Historiographical Problem," *American Historical Review* 91, no. 3 (June 1986): 519–52.

4. See Guy Devailly, "L'encadrement paroissal: rigueur et insuffisance," in *La réligion populaire en Languedoc du XIIIe siècle à la moitié du XIVe siècle, Cahiers de Fanjeaux* 11 (1976): 387–417.

5. For a clear recent survey of the literature on this problem

Epilogue

from the perspective of medieval history, see Gabrielle M. Spiegel, "History, Historicism and the Social Logic of the Text in the Middle Ages," *Speculum* 65, no. 1 (Jan. 1990): 59–86.

6. The most enthusiastic proponent of the view that the two were connected was Steven Runciman, *The Medieval Manichee* (Cambridge, 1947).

7. Adhemar of Chabannes, "'Manichaeans' in Aquitaine," trans. Walter L. Wakefield and Austin P. Evans, in *Heresies of the High Middle Ages*, ed. Wakefield and Evans (New York and London, 1969), no. 2, 74.

8. D. Obolensky, *The Byzantine Commonwealth* (London, 1971), 113; quoted by Robert I. Moore in *The Origins of European Dissent* (London, 1977), 155.

9. D. Angelov, *Le Bogomilisme en Bulgarie*, trans. L. Petrova-Boinay (Toulouse, 1972), 24–25; quoted in Moore, *Origins*, 155.

10. The text is called "The Secret Supper." It exists in two European copies. Wakefield and Evans, *Heresies*, includes an English translation, no. 56, 458–65; the passage on taxes is on page 459. See also Moore, *Origins*, 161–63.

11. Eberwin's letter is translated by Wakefield and Evans, *Heresies*, no. 15, 126–32.

12. See the discussion in Moore, *Origins*, esp. 197–200.

13. The letter is translated by Wakefield and Evans, *Heresies*, no. 14, 122.

14. *Patrologia Latina*, vol. 185, col. 313.

15. Geoffrey II, bishop of Chartres, "Epistola ad Archenfredum," *Patrologia Latina*, vol. 185, col. 411.

16. See A. P. Evans's classic and still very useful essay "Social Aspects of Medieval Heresy," in *Persecution and Liberty: Essays in Honour of George Lincoln Burr* (New York, 1931), 3–20. There is a brief but valuable discussion in *Hérésies et sociétés dans l'Europe pré-industrielle, 11e–18e siècles*, ed. Jacques LeGoff (Paris, 1968), 278–80.

17. Geoffrey II, "Epistola ad Archenfredum," col. 412.

18. See Pierre Bonnassie, "Du Rhône à la Galice: Genèse et modalités du régime féodal," in *Structures féodales et féodalisme dans*

l'Occident méditerranéen (Xe–XIIIe siècles), Collection de l'école française de Rome, 44 (1980), 18–44.

19. Archibald Lewis, "La féodalité dans le Toulousain et la France méridionale (850–1050)," *Annales du Midi* 76 (1964): 247–59.

20. Bonnassie argues in "Du Rhône à la Galice" that this was the period of the development of feudal terminology and relations in Languedoc: the knights owed military service and loyalty to their lord, in exchange for a fief, a means of support.

21. Paul Ourliac, "La féodalité méridionale," in *Les pays de la Méditerranée occidentale au moyen âge: Etudes et recherches, Actes du 106e congrès national des sociétés savantes, Perpignan, 1981* (Paris, 1983), 7–11; Ourliac, "Réalité ou imaginaire: la féodalité toulousaine," in *Religion, société et politique: Mélanges en homage à Jacques Ellul* (Paris, 1983), 331–44.

22. Thomas Bisson, "The Organized Peace in S. France and Catalonia," reprinted in his book *Medieval France and Her Pyrenean Neighbours* (Ronceverte, W.V., 1989), 215–36.

23. On Languedocian villages, see the thesis of Monique Bourin-Derruau, *Villages médiévaux en bas-Languedoc: Genèse d'une sociabilité, Xe–XIVe siècle* (Paris, 1987); on the rural consulate, see 1:311–13.

24. Quoted in Moore, *Origins*, 197–98.

25. Wakefield and Evans, *Heresies*, 703n.

26. On the problems raised by this text, see Jean Duvernoy, *L'histoire de cathares* (Toulouse, 1979), 2:209–13.

27. The upper clergy included the archbishop of Narbonne and the bishops of Albi, Toulouse, Nimes, Lodève, and Agde.

28. Wakefield and Evans, *Heresies*, no. 28, 191–92.

29. Bernard Hamilton, "The Cathar Council of Saint-Felix," Appendix to Moore, *Origins*, 285–89. A French translation of much of the text appears in Duvernoy, *L'histoire des cathares*, 2:216–18.

30. See Moore, *Origins*, 212.

31. See Wakefield and Evans, *Heresies*, no. 23, 161.

32. "Epistola Cardinalis," quoted in the "Gesta regis Henrici secundi Benedicti abatis," ed. William Stubbs, in *The Chronicle of*

the Reigns of Henry II and Richard I, A.D. *1169–1192* (London, 1867), 1:203.

33. The "debt of marriage" meant sexual relations.

34. The abjuration was that of Berengar of Tours in 1059; see John Mundy, "Noblesse et hérésie. Une famille cathare: Les Maurand," *Annales ESC* 29 (1974): 1222–23.

35. For this information and a very detailed reconstruction of the Maurand family, see John Mundy, *The Repression of Catharism at Toulouse: The Royal Diploma of 1279* (Toronto, 1985), 229–41.

36. See Richard Abels and Ellen Harrison, "The Participation of Women in Languedocian Catharism," *Medieval Studies* 41 (1979): 215–51.

37. Walter L. Wakefield, in *Heresy, Crusade and Inquisition in Southern France, 1100–1250* (Berkeley and Los Angeles, 1974), reviewed the older estimates and arrived at this very rough figure.

38. See Elie Griffe, *Le Languedoc cathare* (Paris, 1980), esp. 83–89, 99, 119–21, 124, 128–30, 134, 136, 141, 149, 174–75; for reconverts to Catharism, see 105, 144, 127. See also Malcom Lambert, "The Motives of the Cathars: Some Reflections," *Studies in Church History* 15 (1978): 55.

39. Wakefield, *Heresy, Crusade and Inquisition,* 70; he cites Dossat, "Cathares et vaudois à la veille de la croisade albigeoise," *Revue historique et littéraire de Languedoc* 3 (1946): 79.

40. See the discussion in Wakefield, *Heresy, Crusade and Inquisition,* 70–71; he cites Jean Duvernoy, "Guilhabert de Castres" and "Bertrand Marty," *Cahiers d'études cathares,* 2d ser., 28, no. 34 (1967): 32–42, and 2d ser., 29, no. 39 (1968): 19–35.

41. Quoted in Peter Dronke, *Women Writers of the Middle Ages* (Cambridge, 1984), 210; the Latin text is given on 269–70.

42. This is an unpublished case from Orvieto; Archivio di Stato di Orvieto, Liber Inquisitionis, 24 recto.

43. Mundy, *Repression.*

44. For these estimates, see Mundy, *Repression,* 48.

45. Quoted in Mundy, *Repression,* 41.

46. Quoted in Mundy, *Repression,* 25n.

47. There is a very large literature on this general movement.

One classic study that connects twelfth-century theology with apostolic movements is Marie-Dominic Chenu, *Nature, Man and Society in the Twelfth Century* (Paris, 1957; English trans. by Jerome Taylor and Lester Little, Chicago and London, 1968). Lester Little argued in 1978 that the movement for apostolic poverty was connected to the rise of a profit economy; see his *Religious Poverty and the Profit Economy in Medieval Europe* (London, 1978).

48. Lambert, "Motives," 49–59.

49. Mundy espouses this view; see *Repression*, 9. See also John Mundy, *Men and Women at Toulouse in the Age of the Cathars* (Toronto, 1990), 3.

50. Jacques Chiffoleau, "Vie et mort de l'hérésie en Provence et dans la vallée du Rhône du début du XIIIe au début du XIVe siècle," in *Effacement du Catharisme? (XIIIe–XIVe siècle), Cahiers de Fanjeaux* 20 (1985): 73–99.

51. Quoted in Chiffoleau, "Vie et mort," 77.

52. Mundy, *Men and Women*, 53.

53. Wakefield, *Heresy, Crusade and Inquisition*, 72.

54. Mundy, *Liberty and Political Power in Toulouse, 1100–1230* (New York, 1952), 81–82.

55. The text is quoted in Mundy, *Repression*, 25.

56. On the formation of lineages see David Herlihy, *Medieval Households* (Cambridge, Mass., 1985), chap. 4.

57. On the movement of women into religious life, see Brenda Bolton, "Mulieres sanctae," in *Sanctity and Secularity: The Church and the World*, ed. Derek Baker, Studies in Church History 10 (New York, 1973), 77–95. On the shift to Roman dowries, see Diane Hughes, "From Brideprice to Dowry in Mediterranean Europe," *Journal of Family History* 3 (1978): 262–96.

58. The story is told by Mundy, *Men and Women*, 42.

59. The text is MS. 609 of the Bibliothèque Municipale of Toulouse. See also Abels and Harrison, "Participation of Women."

60. Griffe thought that this was more common; see *Le Languedoc cathare*, 26–27.

61. Her testimony is quoted in Mundy, *Men and Women*, 42.

62. Mundy, *Repression*, 178–90.

63. "The Chronicle of William Pelhisson," trans. Walter L. Wakefield, in *Heresy, Crusade and Inquisition,* 213. Wakefield's translation is based on a fourteenth-century copy of the lost original, edited by C. Douais in *Les sources de l'histoire de l'Inquisition dans le Midi de la France au XIIIe et XIVe siècles* (Paris, 1881), 81–118.

64. Wakefield and Evans print them in translation; see *Heresies,* nos. 56–60, 447–630.

65. Wakefield states that one witness reported this as "sed erat bestia," the other as "stulta"; he translates it as "nincompoop." I suspect that in the original, spoken Occitan, Garcias was likening believers such as William and Ayma to mindless animals.

66. This text was published by Céléstin Douais, *Documents pour servir à l'histoire de l'Inquisition dans le Languedoc* (Paris, 1900), 2:90–114. The English translation excerpted here is from Wakefield, *Heresy, Crusade and Inquisition,* 242–49.

67. See Emmanuel Le Roy Ladurie, *Montaillou: The Promised Land of Error* (New York, 1978).

68. The register was edited by Jean Duvernoy, though with some errors. These accounts were translated from the original text by Peter Dronke in *Women Writers of the Middle Ages,* 205–15. Dronke prints the Latin original in an appendix, with his emendations of Duvernoy's edition noted.

APPENDIXES

Excerpts from Cathar Rituals

We have two versions of Cathar rituals: one in Occitan, one in Latin. The Latin version is longer, but the basic ceremonies are the same. There is some reason to believe that the Occitanian text is older than the Latin. In any case, it seemed best to use the version that would have been most familiar to the people of Occitania.

Both versions have been translated into modern European languages many times. The latest complete English translation is in *Heresies of the High Middle Ages,* by Walter L. Wakefield and Austin P. Evans (New York, 1969). I have made my own translation, but almost every word of it has been anticipated by one or another of my predecessors. All I could do was to try for clarity, consistency, and euphony.

Two points of doctrine should be emphasized. The Cathars often put the word "supersubstantial" before "bread" in the prayer "Give us this day our daily bread." If "supersubstantial" were not inserted in the prayer, the word was introduced elsewhere, in Cathar sermons and commentaries, for example. The idea, of course, was that a believer should not pray for a material and therefore evil benefit, and that "bread" meant the spiritual food, the saving doctrine brought by Christ. The other point is that to the Cathars baptism by water was useless, if not sinful. The only real baptism was baptism by the Spirit, which came with the laying on of hands.

243

The Transmission of the Lord's Prayer

If the believer has fasted and if the Christians [the perfect] have agreed to admit him to the Prayer, let them wash their hands, and such believers as are there shall do likewise. And then the leading Good Man [perfect], the one who ranks after the elder, shall make three bows to the elder and then prepare a table. Let him bow again three times; then let him spread a cloth on the table and again bow thrice. Then he shall put the Book [the Gospels] on the table and say: *"Bless us, have mercy on us."*[1] Then let the believer perform his *melioramentum*[2] and take the Book from the hand of the elder. And the elder should admonish him and preach to him from suitable texts. [Here follow verses from the New Testament, beginning with: "When two or three of you are gathered together in My Name, I shall be in the midst of you."] "From all this you must understand that in presenting yourself before the sons of Jesus Christ, you are confirming the faith and the teaching of the Church of God, as the Holy Scriptures give us to understand. For the people of God deserted the Lord God long ago. They

---

[1] Italicized phrases are in Latin in the original, and are phrases repeated at frequent intervals by the congregation.

[2] This act consisted in bowing or genuflecting three times before one of the "perfect," saying "Bless us, have mercy on us," and receiving a benediction. The Catholics called this "adoring" the heretical leader, and considered performing the *melioramentum* one of the surest signs of heresy. Thus it might be dangerous to bow to a heretic, even if one did so only out of courtesy.

departed from the wisdom and the will of their Divine Father, deceived by evil spirits and submitting themselves to them. And for these and many other reasons you must understand that Our Father wishes to have pity on his people and to receive them into His peace and harmony through the coming of His Son, Jesus Christ. Therefore you are here in the presence of the disciples of Jesus Christ, in this place, where, as was shown before, the Father, Son, and Holy Ghost dwell in spirit, so that you may receive the holy prayer that the Lord Jesus Christ gave to his disciples and so that your petitions and your prayers may be heard by Our Father. You must understand that if you wish to receive this holy prayer you must repent for all your sins and forgive all men. . . . Moreover, if God gives you grace to receive this holy prayer, you should vow in your heart that you will keep it all the days of your life, according to the custom of the Church of God, in truth and chastity and in all other good virtues which God may vouchsafe you. We therefore pray the Good Lord, who made the disciples of Jesus Christ worthy to receive and hold to this holy prayer, that He will give to you also the grace of receiving and holding to it, for His honor and for your salvation. 'Have mercy on us!' "

And then the elder shall say the prayer and the believer shall repeat it after him. Then let the elder say: "We give you this holy prayer, so that you receive it from God, and from us, and from the Church, and so that you may repeat it at any moment of your life, day and night, alone or in company, and so that you must never eat or drink without first saying this prayer. And if you should fail to do so, you must do penance for your fault." And the believer must answer: "I receive it from God, from you, and from the Church." Then he should perform his *melioramentum* and give thanks. Then let the Christians say a *dobla* [repetitions of the Lord's Prayer] with genuflexions and requests for grace and forgiveness, and the believer shall do the same.

The Consolation

Let the believer perform his *melioramentum* and take the Book from the hand of the elder. And the elder should admonish him and preach to him with suitable texts and in such words as are suitable for a Consolation. Let him speak in this fashion:

"Peter, you wish to receive the spiritual baptism through which the Holy Spirit is given in the Church of God with the holy prayer and the laying on of hands by the Good Men. Our Lord Jesus Christ, speaking of this baptism in the Gospel of St. Matthew, said to his disciples: 'Go forth and teach all nations; baptize them in the name of the Father and of the Son and of the Holy Ghost.' [Many more texts follow; the most important for Cathar doctrine was Acts I, 5: "For John indeed baptized with water, but you shall be baptized with the Holy Spirit."]

"The Church of God has preserved this holy baptism by

which the Holy Spirit is given from the time of the apostles until this day, and it has passed from Good Men to Good Men until now, and the Church will continue to confer it until the end of the world. And you should understand that the Church has power to bind and to loose, to forgive sins and to fix them on men, as Christ said in the Gospel of St. John: 'As the Father sent me forth, I also send you.' And when He had said this, He breathed upon them and said to them: 'Receive the Holy Spirit. If you forgive any men's sins, they are forgiven them, and if you fix any men's sins upon them, they shall remain fixed.' [More texts follow, ending with Luke X, 19: "Behold, I give you power to tread on snakes and on scorpions and upon all the strength of the Enemy, and nothing shall harm you."]

"If you wish to receive this power and this might, you must keep all the commandments of Christ and of the New Testament to the utmost of your ability. Know that He forbade men to commit adultery,[3] to kill,[4] or to lie, to swear oaths[5] or to steal, to do unto others what they would not have done to themselves. He commanded them to forgive those who do evil to them, to love their enemies, to pray for and bless those

---

[3] In strict Cathar doctrine, any act of intercourse, even between man and wife, was adultery.

[4] Self-defense was no excuse for homicide.

[5] The "perfect" could not take oaths even in a court of law; this rule often betrayed them. The early Quakers had somewhat the same problem.

who denounce and accuse them, to turn the other cheek to those who smite them, to give up one's cloak to him who takes away the coat. He forbade them to judge and to condemn. And there are many other commandments that are given by the Lord to His Church.

"Moreover, you must hate this world and its works and all things which are of this world. For Saint John says in his [First] Epistle: 'Beloved, do not love the world, nor the things that are in this world. If anyone loves the world, there is no love for the Father in his heart. For all that is in the world is lust of the flesh, desire of the eyes and pride in life—things that come not from the Father but from the world. And the world and its desires shall pass away, but he who does the will of God shall endure forever.' [More texts follow.] These texts and many others show that you must keep the commandments of God and hate this world. And if you do these things well until the end of your days, we hope that your soul will have eternal life."

Then let the believer say "I have this will. Pray God for me to give me the strength to fulfill it."

Then let the leader of the Good Men make his *melioramentum* with the believer to the elder and say: "*Have mercy on us*. Good Christians, we pray you for the love of God to grant our friend who stands before you this good which God has given you." Then the believer should make his *melioramentum* and say: "*Have mercy on us*. I ask forgiveness from

248

God, from the Church, and from you for all my sins in word
and thought and deed." And the Christians should reply: "May
they be forgiven you by God and by us and by the Church,
and we pray God to forgive you."

When this has been said, let them give him the Consolation. The elder should take the Book [the Gospels] and place
it on the believer's head, and the other Good Men should
touch him with their right hands. Let them say the Pardon,[6]
and the Adoration[7] three times, and then:

*"Our Father, receive thy servant in thy justice and send
thy grace and thy Holy Spirit upon him."*

Then let them say the Prayer to God, and he who leads
the service should recite the Six [repeat the Lord's Prayer six
times] in a low voice. When he has said the Six, he should say
aloud three Adorations and the Prayer and then read the
Gospel [the first verses, probably the first seventeen verses,
of the Gospel of St. John]. When the Gospel has been read,
they should say three Adorations, the Grace,[8] and the Pardon.
Then they should give each other the kiss of peace and kiss the
Book. If there are [simple] believers present, let them exchange

---

[6] The Pardon consisted in saying *"Bless us, have mercy on us"* three
times, and then *"May the Father, Son, and Holy Ghost forgive us all our
sins."*

[7] The Adoration was simply: *"Let us adore the Father, Son, and
Holy Ghost."*

[8] *"May the grace of our Lord Jesus Christ be with you all."*

the kiss of peace also. Let women believers, if any are there, exchange the kiss with each other and kiss the Book. And then let them pray to God with a *dobla*[9] and requests for grace and forgiveness. Thus they will have given [the Consolation].

---

[9] Two repetitions of the Lord's Prayer.

Heresy in Toulouse in 1178: Excerpt from a Letter of Henry, Abbot of Clairvaux

Translated by Hans Hummer with Carol Lansing

This letter is one of two descriptions of the papal legate's mission to Toulouse in 1178; the other was written by the legate himself, Peter of Pavia, cardinal of St. Chrysogono. A third account was compiled from the two letters by an English chronicler in the *Gesta Henrici*, the deeds of the English king Henry II. The author also included the two original letters. There is also a fourth, slightly revised version written by Roger of Hoveden; an English translation appears in Walter L. Wakefield and Austin P. Evans, *Heresies of the High Middle Ages* (New York and London, 1969), 194–200. This text was translated from the edition in the *Gesta Henrici*.[1]

Henry's letter gives us some indication of the popularity of Catharism in Toulouse in 1178. It is also a revealing glimpse of orthodox authorities struggling both to understand

---

[1] "Gesta regis Henrici secundi Benedicti abatis," ed. William Stubbs, in *The Chronicle of the Reigns of Henry II and Richard I, A.D. 1169–1192, Known commonly under the name of Benedict of Peterborough*, Rolls Series 49 (London, 1867), 1:214–20.

the heresy and to root it out. The style of the letter is that of
a twelfth-century monastic author. Like a contemporary sermon, the text is littered with biblical references. A few of
them have been indicated in the notes. These would have
been familiar to Henry's readers and in fact gave them a
context in which to understand what took place. Several
themes run through the letter. Henry was horrified at the
very idea of new doctrine, or a new gospel, which contradicted his whole understanding of the nature of religious
authority. Other recurring themes include the power of words
and the contrast between the light of truth and the darkness
of error. The heretics are moles who dive underground out of
fear of the light. Henry wrote in concrete images and often
evoked the senses: gestures and spoken words are important
to his telling of the story.

The letter begins with a diatribe against heresy, which
has not been translated here. Henry called upon Christians to
lament the appearance of heretics and the injury done to the
salvation of humankind. Then, Henry urged Christian leaders to rise up, as David with his slingshot rose up to defeat
the Philistines. If the church is damaged by heresy it will be
not because her cause lacks truth but from a lack of supporters. He argued that because of the deceptive ways of the
heretics, they could not always be caught. Nevertheless, they
could be driven off and would then perish of themselves. In
this context he recounted his experience in Toulouse. The
end of the letter describes Henry's journey to the diocese of

Albi to confront the viscount Roger Trencavel, while the legate continued his efforts in Toulouse.

For a discussion of the mission to Toulouse and the Maurand family, see the Epilogue.

Recently, at the command of the lord pope and urged by the most pious kings Louis VII of France and Henry II of England, Lord Peter, legate of the apostolic see, visited the city of Toulouse, accompanied by the venerable bishops of Poitou and Bath. I was in the retinue. Toulouse has a numerous population, and it was reported that the city was the mother of heresy and the very source of error. We proceeded to the city in order to learn whether the outcry rising up from the city was because of her suffering.[2] And behold! A great wound was discovered, so that from the sole of her foot to the crown of her head there was scarcely any health in the city.[3] In truth, not even a third of the abominations which that famed city cherished in the bosom of its unbelief had been reported to us. Abomination had found a place of desolation for itself in the city, and like the reptiles described by the prophets had taken up residence in its hiding places.[4] In that city the heretics so ruled over the populace and dominated the clergy that the priests were no different from the people, and the way of life of a pastor was designed

[2] Genesis 18:21.
[3] Numbers 11:33 and Isaiah 1:6.
[4] Daniel 9:27.

for the ruin of his flock.[5] When heretics spoke, everyone marveled, but when it was a Catholic speaking, they said, "Who is this?"[6] If anyone among them dared even to whisper a word of the faith, the rest stupidly drew away from the miracle. The pestilence had so prevailed in the region that the heretics not only made their own priests and popes but even had evangelists. These evangelists distorted and eliminated the true gospel and hammered out new gospels for the people, preaching new doctrines from their wicked hearts to the duped population.

I would mislead you if I did not admit that among them there was a very old and wealthy man, well endowed with kinsmen and friends and great among the most prominent men of the city. This man, urged on by sin, was so blinded by the devil that he called himself John the Evangelist. He distinguished between that Word that was with God in the beginning, and the first cause of material things, as if the first cause derived from another God.[7] He was leader of the damned and chief of the heretics in the city. In this capacity, this man who was a layman and a rustic who knew nothing spewed forth the poisonous fluids of death and damnation among them like a fountain of diabolical wisdom. They flocked to him at night like dark owls. He wore attire resembling the tunic and dalmatica of a priest, and he sat among them like a king surrounded by his army, though he was in

[5] Hosea 4:9.
[6] Matthew 21:10.
[7] John 1:1.

fact a preacher of stupidities. He filled the whole city with his disciples, as no one dared to resist him because of his strength in the city. In fact, when we first made our entrance and traveled directly though the streets and squares, the heretics everywhere enjoyed so much licence that they mocked us with words, pointing with their fingers and calling us "apostates, hypocrites, heretics!"

After time passed and a few days of rest were given us, one of us was ordered to take up the word of exhortation and to debate the rule of the true faith before the faithless multitude. When an orthodox sermon was preached to the people, sinners in Zion were frightened and hypocrites were seized by trembling, so that those who previously had silenced the mouths of speakers now did not dare even to appear before those who spoke.[8] It was as if we heard and saw foxes turn into moles, as those who had previously run about with impunity now dove into their hiding places in the earth and into their hollow caverns.[9] In the bowels of the earth those sacred plants which they dared not keep in the open rotted and died. They also devised a wicked and cunning strategy of pretending to support our position, so that when called for questioning they might pretend to believe whatever we did, lest the discolored leopard betray itself by its different hide.[10]

Consequently, the lord legate, and I and some of the rest

---

[8] Isaiah 33:14.

[9] Isaiah 2:30.

[10] Jeremiah 13:23.

along with him, thought we should meet in the open with these wild beasts, in order to get a good look at those whom fear and confusion had driven ignominiously into the depths of the earth. We directed our zeal and efforts toward forcing them to appear in public so that their works of darkness would be thrust into the light. For this purpose, the legate ordered that the bishop take an oath, along with some of the clergy and consuls of the city, and other faithful men who were not yet touched by any rumor of perfidy, that they would put down for us the names of any active heretics or their supporters of heresy that they had known or might come to know. They were to spare no one for affection, kinship, or money.

In the course of several days, a countless number were placed on the list. Among them was the great Peter Maurand, whom as we said before they call John the Evangelist. We decided in council together to begin a trial against him, so that the rest of the faithless mob would tremble when the simplicity of the true gospel had condemned the wiles of the false evangelist. Accordingly, the Count of St. Gilles, who was loyal to us, sent his officials to Peter Maurand and ordered him to come forward. But Peter Maurand, trusting in his great wealth and numerous relations, by the trick of a needless delay avoided the first summons. The next day the count summoned Peter gently, approaching him through friends and well-known people and cajoling rather than threatening him. At last after many difficulties the count presented Peter to us, using mixed compliments and threats to convince him. Then, one of us spoke and began to warn him in this way: "Come now, Peter, your fellow citizens claim that you challenge the rule of the true faith and have gone over to the wickedness of Arian heresy. You both lead some people astray and are yourself led astray by others, into many errors." In response Peter, sighing deeply and touched at heart by sorrow, at first appearance lied that he was not that sort of person. Asked to prove this with an oath, he claimed that his simple assertion should be believed, since he was a trustworthy and well-known man. When we all persisted in demanding an oath, he immediately promised he would swear. This was done to avoid being detected as a heretic by his obstinance, since it is the custom of the heretics to prohibit oaths. Then, the relics of the saints were respectfully brought forth. The relics were taken up with such solemn reverence and devotion that the faithful were moved to tears and the heretics who were present found they preferred their hiding places to the sight. Peter himself was visibly overcome during the song which we chanted tearfully to invoke the presence of the Holy Spirit. He shuddered and became pale, so that all color and mental strength left him. How could his spirit remain recalcitrant at the coming of the Holy Spirit? He seemed like a man undone by a paralytic disease, unable to speak or feel, though it had been said by all that he was so eloquent that he could speak better than anyone. What more is there to say? While everyone stood by, the unhappy man swore that he would state his true belief concerning any articles of the faith that we asked of him. A miracle took place, during such a spectacle a most welcome pious joy. The book on which Peter had sworn was opened, and one of the bystanders, who in a pious jest searched for a portent, found this verse of Scripture: "What have you to do with us, Jesus, Son of God? Have you come here to torment us before the time?"[11] Truly, Lord Jesus, these men have nothing to do with you whom your heavenly father has cut off from true eternal life, like unproductive branches cast out to wither. But for all of us gathered in your name joy was multiplied and the glory of your goodness resounded in our praise and thanksgiving.

Finally, Peter was simply asked on his oath without any deception to state to us his faith concerning the sacrament of the altar. This was a faith that he did not believe in his heart for the sake of justice or confess with his mouth for the hope of salvation. Instead, he who had always lied about everything now told the truth about his false beliefs. He stated a new doctrine that the holy bread of eternal life, consecrated in the Word of the Lord with the ministry of the priest, was not the body of Christ. Then, everyone surrounded him and, overwhelmed with the tears that his contempt for the sacraments of Christ elicited, reached out to his misery with Christian compassion. Nothing more was needed, they gave

[11] Matthew 8:29.

him over to the count, the accused was judged a criminal and a heretic, and consigned to public custody, placed under the watchful commitment of his relatives. News of the event spread through the streets and squares of this very large city. The mouths of the faithful were opened and the lips of the Catholic people were unloosed in praise of you, O Christ. It was as if the splendor of the faith had burst forth for the first time, and in the hope of eternal salvation the city that just a short time before had despaired now breathed again. From that time the word of the faith increased and multiplied daily, so that the entire appearance of the city seemed more joyful, and escaped from the darkness of error into the clear light of truth.

Meanwhile, Peter reversed himself, moved by the way the Lord cared for him. When he realized that he fully merited death now as well as in the future, he sent many mediators in an effort to find a way to make amends. He promised that he would undergo a conversion, so that he could be freed from the threat of death in order to pursue a better life. He came, he was received, and he was made to stand naked in view of the surrounding people, as he stripped off the evil of his old bad faith. There he acknowledged his heresy before all; there he gave his hand to the faith; there he renounced error. His guarantors were not only the count himself but many of the foremost of his fellow citizens. Peter took the oath with his right hand before all that he submitted to every order of the lord legate and would fulfill his promise in all things. Then, it was announced to the people so that all could equally congregate at the church of Saint-Sernin on the next day, in order to hear and see with solemnity what form of penance Peter was to take upon himself. The following day, because they had been forewarned, a great multitude gathered. It was so crowded that without a lot of pressing together there scarcely remained enough space around the altar for the papal legate to celebrate mass. And behold! Before that immense crowd, Peter, now one of us, was led naked and barefoot through the very doors of the church. The bishop of Toulouse and the abbot of Saint-Sernin scourged him on either side until he was prostrate at the feet of the legate on the steps of the altar. There in the front of the church he abjured all heresy and anathematized heretics and was reconciled through the sacraments of the church. Immediately afterwards, his possessions were confiscated and appropriated for public use. Penance was imposed on him: within forty days he was to be exiled from his homeland and to take himself away and serve the poor of Jerusalem for three years. In the meantime, every Sunday he was to make a circuit of the churches of Toulouse, naked and barefoot, scourged with rods. He was to return all the wealth he had taken from the church, to repay all the usurious interest he had charged, and to make reparations to the poor whom he had ill-treated. A certain *castrum* he owned, which had been profaned by gatherings of heretics, was to be destroyed to the foundation.

God of goodness! So many tears of holy joy were shed for you! What praises and thanksgivings the devoted, rejoicing people poured forth to the heavens with singing and dancing, since such a mole was pulled from the caves of perfidy, and a savage wolf was reformed into a lamb of Israel!

Bibliographical Note

Almost all contemporary chroniclers in Western European countries had something to say about the Albigensian Crusades, but three wrote books devoted entirely to this subject. Pierre des Vaux-de-Cernay, nephew of Gui, bishop of Carcassonne, wrote a *Historia Albigensis* which covers the Crusades down to the death of Simon de Montfort. It is pro-French, pro-Montfort, but quite accurate on details. The best edition is by P. Guébin and E. Lyon, in three volumes (1926–1939). The *Chanson de la croisade contre les Albigeois,* begun by Guillaume de Tudèle and continued by an anonymous writer for the period 1213–1219, was written from a southern point of view. Guillaume was strongly Catholic, but rather hostile to the French; his anonymous continuator was an Occitanian patriot who gloried in Montfort's defeats. There is an excellent edition by E. Martin-Chabot (1931–1957) and another that is quite usable by Paul Meyer (1875–1879). Finally, there is the briefer and not quite contemporary *Cronica* of Guillaume de Puylaurens, a native of the South and a notary for the Inquisition. There is no entirely satisfactory edition of this work; it may be found most easily in the *Recueil des historiens des Gaules et de la France,* vols. XIX, 193–235, XX, 764–776.

Papal letters are of great importance. Those of all the popes of the period have been calendared. Innocent III's letters were published in the *Patrologia Latina* CCXIV–CCXVII, and some of Honorius' appear in the collection of his works edited by C. A. Horoy. The acts of church councils, especially local councils, are helpful; they may be found in J. D. Mansi, *Sacrorum conciliorum collectia.* There is surprisingly little about Occitanian problems in the letters of Philip Augustus, Louis VIII, and St. Louis. There is also surprisingly little material about conditions in the South in the period 1200–1250 in the great *Histoire générale de Languedoc* by C. Devic and J. Vaissete (the revised edition by A. Molinier should be used), though vol. VIII does include a catalogue of the acts of Raymond VI and Raymond VII and letters of Simon de Montfort. But one of the great problems in writing about the Albigensian Crusades is that evidence becomes abundant only in the second half of the thirteenth century, when pressures by the French royal government and by the Inquisition were transforming southern society. The best stories about evil priests and zealous heretics, and the fullest descriptions of Cathar beliefs and rituals, all come from this late period. Historians have assumed that this evidence can be used to describe conditions in the early thirteenth century, but this assumption is a little risky.

There is an excellent collection of original sources concerning Waldensian and Cathar beliefs in W. L. Wakefield and A. P. Evans, *Heresies of the High Middle Ages* (1969). A convenient collection in French, which duplicates many of the documents in Wakefield and Evans, is R. Nelli, *Ecritures cathares* (1959). For the Inquisition C. Douais edited in 1900 some documents illustrating its practices about the middle of the thirteenth century, and G. Mollat published Bernard Gui's *Manuel de l'Inquisiteur* (1926–1927), which describes conditions about half a century later.

There is surprisingly little in English about the Albigensian Crusades. The best account is by Austin P. Evans in volume II of *A History of the Crusades* (ed. Kenneth M. Setton, 1962). Zoë Oldenbourg's *Massacre at Montségur: a History of the Albigensian Crusade* (1961) is lively reading, but is strongly prejudiced in favor of the heretics. Jacques Madaule, *The Albigensian Crusade* (1967) is not very satisfactory. John Mundy's *Liberty and Political Power in Toulouse* (1954) gives a good description of social and political conditions in the city, but has little to say about the war. In French, A. Luchaire, *Innocent III: la Croisade des Albigeois* (1905) is a good account of papal policy. Pierre Belperron, *La Croisade contre les Albigeois* (1942) is full of solid factual detail, but shows some bias in favor of the crusaders and the submergence of Languedoc into France. The Crusades of Louis VIII are admirably described by Charles Petit-Dutaillis in his *Etude sur la vie et le règne de Louis VIII* (1894).

The Inquisition has fascinated many historians. The pioneer work of Henry Charles Lea, *A History of the Inquisition of the Middle Ages* (3 vols., 1888), shows all the prejudices of a liberal, anticlerical writer, but it contains a vast amount of useful material. R. W. Emery has written a good case study in *Heresy and the Inquisition in Narbonne* (1941). Jean Guiraud has given an orthodox but reasonably fair treatment of the institution in *The Mediaeval Inquisition* (1929). Those who can read French will prefer his later and longer work, *Histoire de l'Inquisition au moyen âge* (2 vols., 1935–1938). The older work of E. Vacandard, *The Inquisition* (1908), written from a strongly Catholic point of view, is still useful.

Supplemental English Language Bibliography

The most up-to-date history of medieval heresy in English is now Malcolm Lambert's *Medieval Heresy: Popular Movements from the Gregorian Reform to the Reformation*, second edition (Cambridge, 1992). For early medieval heresy, see Robert I. Moore, *The Origins of European Dissent* (London, 1977); for later heresy, Gordon Leff, *Heresy in the Later Middle Ages* (New York, 1967). For heresy understood in the context of the rise of persecution, see Robert I. Moore, *The Formation of a Persecuting Society* (Oxford, 1987). Edward Peters's *Heresy and Authority in the Middle Ages* (London, 1980) is a useful textbook with translated documents. Other fine collections of documents include Robert I. Moore, *The Birth of Popular Heresy* (London, 1980) and Walter Wakefield and A. P. Evans, *Heresies of the High Middle Ages* (New York, 1969). There are very useful published bibliographies on medieval heresy, including Carl T. Berkhout and Jeffrey B. Russell, *Medieval Heresies: A Bibliography, 1960–1979* (Toronto, 1981) and a bibliography published by H. Grundmann and reprinted in *Hérésies et sociétés dans l'Europe pré-industrielle, 11e–18e siècles,* ed. Jacques LeGoff (Paris, 1968). For articles published since 1979, the reader should consult a serial bibliography in medieval studies that includes heresy: the *International Medieval Bibliography* (Leeds, Eng., 1967–).

On southern French heresy, Walter Wakefield, *Heresy, Crusade and Inquisition in Southern France, 1100–1250* (Berkeley and Los Angeles, 1974) is a good general history. Several specialized studies of southern France in English treat heresy in part, including Emmanuel Le Roy Ladurie's *Montaillou: The Promised Land of Error* (New York, 1978), John Mundy's *The Repression of Catharism at Toulouse: The Royal Diploma of 1279* (Toronto, 1985), and Mundy's *Men and Women at Toulouse in the Age of the Cathars* (Toronto, 1990).

There is a large bibliography on the repression of heresy. On the Inquisition, see Bernard Hamilton, *The Medieval Inquisition* (London, 1981) and the classic by H. C. Lea, *A History of the Inquisition of the Middle Ages*, especially volume 3, *The Inquisition in the Several Lands of Christendom* (1906–7; rpt., New York, 1955). A recent study explores the efforts of the French state to impose control in Languedoc after the crusades: James Given, *State and Society in Medieval Europe* (Ithaca, N.Y., 1990).

Students interested in Languedocian Catharism and able to read French could begin with the many volumes of the *Cahiers de Fanjeaux*, especially vol. 14, *Historiographie du Catharisme* (1979), and vol. 20, *Effacement du catharisme? (XIIIe–XIVe s.)* (1985), for guides to the bibliography.

Index

INDEX

Castles, 7, 11, 59, 64, 69, 70, 71, 80–83, 99, 102, 119, 152, 167. *See also* Strongholds

Catalan, 3

Catalonia, 88–89

Cathar Church, 26–34, 80; rituals, 32–34, 175–182; underground, 140–141, 143, 151–162

Catharism, 15–16, 26–39, 41–49, 60, 65, 71, 73, 80–81, 90, 99, 140–144, 146–147, 150, 152, 158–159, 172; fidelity to, 160; in Italy, 49; sympathizers of, 34, 61, 99, 143. *See also* Inquisition

Catholicism, ix, 21–22, 30–32, 34–35, 38–39, 42–43, 48, 55, 60–62, 65–67, 70–71, 80, 88, 91, 102, 145, 153, 161. *See also* Roman Catholic Church

Champagne, 2, 16, 45; count of, 116, 133

Charity, 36

Charlemagne, 132, 171

Charles of Anjou, 165

Chastity, 17–18, 30, 35

Château Narbonnais, 112

Children, 62–63, 112, 118

Christ, 22, 29, 69; humanity of, 27. *See also* Real presence

Christendom, 21, 24, 27, 52, 90. *See also* Roman Catholic Church

Christians: disobedient, 43; early, 33, 34, 37

Church-State relations, 20, 149, 151–152, 173–174

Cistercian Order, 41, 43

Cîteaux, 41; abbot of, 41. *See also* Amaury, Arnaud

Cities/states, 7, 13, 49, 96, 99, 108, 131, 146, 165

Citizenship, 7

Civil war, 47

Clairvaux, 25, 40

Clement V, Pope, 44, 162

Clergy, 4–7, 16, 87–88, 127; appointments, 17, 20, 21; in Béziers massacre, 62–63; charges against, 16–19, 37; and crown, 116–117, 138, 164–165; in Crusades, 52; of England, 20; forbidden to shed blood, 149–150; illiteracy of, 17–19; income of, 5–6, 16–17, 18; and the Inquisition, 147n; lower, 17–18; among mountain lords, 12; patrons of, 17; power and privileges of, 4–7, 12, 16–19, 36, 72, 87, 96, 99–100, 116, 126–128, 147, 170; removed, 17, 19, 90; in towns, 5–7; upper, 4, 5, 12, 19–20, 50. *See also* Legates, papal

Cluny, 24

Cologne, 3; archbishop of, 21

Comminges, 105; count of, 82, 84–85, 91, 99, 105, 111–112, 116

Communications, 85, 93

Communion, 150. *See also* Meal, communal

Compromise, 168

Comptes, Chambres de, 166

Concubinage, 17–18

Confiscation, 65, 66, 89, 149–150, 155–159, 160. *See also* Landholdings, lost by conquest and seizure

Conquests, x, xii, 10, 48, 56, 68, 72, 73, 79, 84–85, 90, 92, 98 100–102, 106, 116, 119–120, 124–125, 134–140, 142–143, 167, 173–174

Conrad IV of Marburg, 13

Consecrated ground, 120–121, 156

Consolation, rite of, 33

Constance, mother of Baldwin, 97n

Constance, queen of Sicily, 46

Consuls, 7

Contempt, public, 149

INDEX

Faith: abjuring, 71, 141, 146, 147, 153, 159; defending the true, 42–43, 56, 69, 95, 146; loss of, xii, xiii, 21, 24, 173–174. *See also* Crusades; Inquisition

Fealty, 8, 69, 71, 73, 77, 79, 80–81, 85, 87, 101, 108, 115, 120, 124, 130, 138, 140, 171. *See also* Service, feudal; Vassals

Feast days, solemn, 59

Fee, burial, 17

Fiefs, 12, 46, 52, 54*n*, 67, 73, 76–77, 84, 86, 87, 96, 99, 103, 109*n*, 122, 163; of the church, 99–100; of the crown, 52, 101, 156–157. *See also* Landholdings, lost by conquest and seizure

Fines, 111, 130, 162. *See also* Confiscations; Penalties

Fire, death by: during Crusades, 71, 75, 80, 141, 143; under Inquisition, 149, 150–151, 157, 158, 162

Flanders, 2, 3, 161

Florence, 147

Foix, count of (to 1223, Raymond Roger of Foix), 12, 47, 56, 69, 70, 78, 81–84, 91, 94, 96, 97, 99, 105, 111–112, 116, 120–121. *See also* (after 1223) Roger Bernard

Food, 133

Foot-soldier, 63

Force, armed, 42–52, 134, 135, 138

Fortresses. *See* Castles; Strongholds; Towns, fortified

Forty-day crusaders, 53, 70, 72, 80, 133

France, Ile de, 1, 3, 16, 69, 98, 101, 170

France, northern, ix–xiii, 1–11, 15–16, 18, 21, 25, 44–47, 52, 54–56, 59–61, 66–67, 74, 84, 88, 92, 167; conquests and exactions, x, xii, 10, 103, 129–139; court of,

France, northern (*Cont.*)
10*n*, 97, 97*n*; role in Crusades, 46, 48–49, 78, 88, 106, 112–116, 123–142; homogeneity of, 2, 170–171; kings of, 47, 81, 117, 125, 173–174; origins, 1–3; relationship with papacy of, 138, 156–157, 159, 173–174; rise to power of, xiii, 100–101, 131, 137–139, 142, 167, 169, 173–174; royal house of, x–xi, 2, 48–49, 101–102, 107, 117, 119. *See also* Capetians; France, Ile de; Louis VIII; Louis IX; Philip II; Royal domain; Service, feudal; Treaty of Paris

France, southern, ix–x, 2–11, 48–72, 164–174; affinities, 3, 8, 9, 11, 13, 14, 88, 89, 112–114; economics of, 4–5, 7–8, 89; fragmentation of landholdings, 4–5, 138; military fragmentation, 69–70, 83–84; political fragmentation, xiii, 4–7, 10–12, 14, 15, 20, 25, 56, 84*n*, 88*n*, 89, 96, 99–100, 138; secularism, political, x–xii, 20, 25; service, feudal, 89; urbanism, 7–8. *See also* Dynasts, local; Languedoc; Occitania; Toulouse; Towns; Unity

Francis, St., 36, 37

Franciscan Order, 147*n*

Frangipani family, 128

Franks, 1–2

Frederick I (Barbarossa), 43

Frederick II, 45, 46, 103, 127

French: domination, spread of, 50, 73, 79, 86–88, 90, 92, 96–97, 106, 108, 114–115, 122, 124, 127, 131, 134, 137–143, 151, 161–174; families, in South, 73, 88; foothold in Italy, 173; language, 3, 9, 16, 167, 169; law,

273

INDEX

INDEX

INDEX

Vassals (*Cont.*)
    dispossessed, 93; of king, 138;
    noble, x, 7, 11, 14, 47, 49, 56,
    59, 65, 82, 85–89, 91, 129, 164;
    of Peter II, 89, 91; of Raymond
    VII, 140; of Simon de Montfort,
    86–88, 106; of towns, 7–8, 93
Villages, 6, 7, 53
Viollet-le-Duc, 64
Viviers, bishop of, 12, 19
Vows, 49, 57, 74, 76, 79, 136, 145;
    by crusaders, 43–44, 46, 48, 53,
    101, 114*n*. *See also* Oath-taking

Wages, soldiers', 69
Waldensianism, 15, 26, 36–39, 61,
    143, 154–155, 162
Waldo, Peter, 15, 36–37

War, 7, 10, 11, 47, 53, 69, 74, 104,
    107, 108, 116–117, 136, 139,
    143, 161, 172
War chest, 130
Warfare, medieval. *See* Campaigns;
    Crusades; Sieges
Wars, holy, xi, 11–13, 43–53, 166–
    168
Water supply, 65, 80, 113
Wealth, 6, 13. *See also* Landhold-
    ings; Languedoc; Normandy
Weather, 113, 133–134, 141
West. *See* Europe
Women, 22, 28, 30, 32, 37, 62–63,
    71, 80, 112, 114, 115, 118, 141
World, evil of, 26

Zara 67

283

Ann Arbor Paperbacks

Waddell, *The Desert Fathers*
Erasmus, *The Praise of Folly*
Donne, *Devotions*
Malthus, *Population: The First Essay*
Berdyaev, *The Origin of Russian Communism*
Einhard, *The Life of Charlemagne*
Edwards, *The Nature of True Virtue*
Gilson, *Héloïse and Abélard*
Aristotle, *Metaphysics*
Kant, *Education*
Boulding, *The Image*
Duckett, *The Gateway to the Middle Ages* (3 vols.): *Italy; France and Britain; Monasticism*
Bowditch and Ramsland, *Voices of the Industrial Revolution*
Luxemburg, *The Russian Revolution* and *Leninism or Marxism?*
Rexroth, *Poems from the Greek Anthology*
Zoshchenko, *Scenes from the Bathhouse*
Thrupp, *The Merchant Class of Medieval London*
Procopius, *Secret History*
Adcock, *Roman Political Ideas and Practice*
Swanson, *The Birth of the Gods*
Xenophon, *The March Up Country*
Trotsky, *The New Course*
Buchanan and Tullock, *The Calculus of Consent*
Hobson, *Imperialism*
Pobedonostsev, *Reflections of a Russian Statesman*
Kinietz, *The Indians of the Western Great Lakes 1615–1760*
Bromage, *Writing for Business*
Lurie, *Mountain Wolf Woman, Sister of Crashing Thunder*
Leonard, *Baroque Times in Old Mexico*
Meier, *Negro Thought in America, 1880–1915*
Burke, *The Philosophy of Edmund Burke*
Michelet, *Joan of Arc*
Conze, *Buddhist Thought in India*
Arberry, *Aspects of Islamic Civilization*
Chesnutt, *The Wife of His Youth and Other Stories*
Gross, *Sound and Form in Modern Poetry*
Zola, *The Masterpiece*
Chesnutt, *The Marrow of Tradition*
Aristophanes, *Four Comedies*
Aristophanes, *Three Comedies*
Chesnutt, *The Conjure Woman*
Duckett, *Carolingian Portraits*
Rapoport and Chammah, *Prisoner's Dilemma*
Aristotle, *Poetics*
Peattie, *The View from the Barrio*
Duckett, *Death and Life in the Tenth Century*
Langford, *Galileo, Science and the Church*
McNaughton, *The Taoist Vision*

Anderson, *Matthew Arnold and the Classical Tradition*
Milio, *9226 Kercheval*
Weisheipl, *The Development of Physical Theory in the Middle Ages*
Breton, *Manifestoes of Surrealism*
Gershman, *The Surrealist Revolution in France*
Burt, *Mammals of the Great Lakes Region*
Scholz, *Carolingian Chronicles*
Wik, *Henry Ford and Grass-roots America*
Sahlins and Service, *Evolution and Culture*
Wickham, *Early Medieval Italy*
Waddell, *The Wandering Scholars*
Rosenberg, *Bolshevik Visions* (2 parts in 2 vols.)
Mannoni, *Prospero and Caliban*
Aron, *Democracy and Totalitarianism*
Shy, *A People Numerous and Armed*
Taylor, *Roman Voting Assemblies*
Hesiod, *The Works and Days; Theogony; The Shield of Herakles*
Raverat, *Period Piece*
Lamming, *In the Castle of My Skin*
Fisher, *The Conjure-Man Dies*
Strayer, *The Albigensian Crusades*
Lamming, *The Pleasures of Exile*
Lamming, *Natives of My Person*
Glaspell, *Lifted Masks and Other Works*
Grand, *The Heavenly Twins*
Cornford, *The Origin of Attic Comedy*
Allen, *Wolves of Minong*
Brathwaite, *Roots*
Fisher, *The Walls of Jericho*
Lamming, *The Emigrants*
Loudon, *The Mummy!*
Kemble and Butler Leigh, *Principles and Privilege*
Thomas, *Out of Time*
Flanagan, *You Alone Are Dancing*
Kotre and Hall, *Seasons of Life*
Shen, *Almost a Revolution*
Meckel, *Save the Babies*
Laver and Schofield, *Multiparty Government*
Rutt, *The Bamboo Grove*
Endelman, *The Jews of Georgian England, 1714–1830*
Lamming, *Season of Adventure*
Radin, *Crashing Thunder*
Mirel, *The Rise and Fall of an Urban School System*
Brainard, *When the Rainbow Goddess Wept*
Brook, *Documents on the Rape of Nanking*
Mendel, *Vision and Violence*
Hymes, *Reinventing Anthropology*
Mulroy, *Early Greek Lyric Poetry*
Siegel, *The Rope of God*
Buss, *La Patera*